TEACHER'S PET PUBLICATIONS

LitPlan Teacher Pack
for
INTO THE WILD
based on the book by
Jon Krakauer

Copyright 2013 Teacher's Pet Publications
All Rights Reserved

ISBN 978-1-60249-401-5

Copyright Teacher's Pet Publications 2013

Reproduction of this publication is limited to one single-teacher, single-classroom license. Photocopying of this copyrighted product is permissible for one teacher for his or her own classroom use only.

No part of this publication may be translated, stored in a retrieval system, or transmitted, distributed, posted, displayed or shared in any way or by any means (electronic, digital, mechanical, photocopying, recording, or otherwise) without prior written permission from Teacher's Pet Publications.

Reproduction of any part of this publication for multiple school terms, an entire school or for a school system, by for-profit institutions and tutoring centers, or for commercial sale is strictly prohibited.

For any additional copyright questions,
contact Teacher's Pet Publications.

www.tpet.com

TABLE OF CONTENTS *Into The Wild*

Introduction	5
Unit Objectives	8
Reading Assignment Sheet	9
Unit Outline	10
Short Answer Questions	13
Multiple Choice Questions	25
Vocabulary Worksheets	51
Daily Lessons	73
Nonfiction Assignment	85
Oral Reading Evaluation	92
Writing Assignment 1	81
Writing Evaluation Form	82
Writing Assignment 2	94
Writing Assignment 3	111
Discussion Questions	109
Vocabulary Review	112
Unit Review	117
Unit Tests	123
Unit Resource Materials	163
Vocabulary Resource Materials	179

ABOUT THE AUTHOR

Jon Krakauer

Born in 1954, Jon Krakauer grew up in Corvallis, Oregon, where his father introduced him to mountaineering as an eight-year-old. After graduating from Hampshire College in 1976, Krakauer divided his time between Colorado, Alaska, and the Pacific Northwest, supporting himself primarily as a carpenter and commercial salmon fisherman. For the next two decades, however, his life revolved around climbing mountains.

In 1996 Krakauer climbed Mt. Everest, but a storm took the lives of four of the five teammates who reached the summit with him. An analysis of the calamity he wrote for *Outside* magazine received a National Magazine Award. The unsparingly forthright book he subsequently wrote about Everest, *Into Thin Air*, became a #1 New York Times bestseller and was translated into more than twenty-five languages. It was also Time magazine's Book of the Year, and was one of three finalists for the Pulitzer Prize.

In 1998, as a tribute to his companions lost on Everest, Krakauer established the Everest '96 Memorial Fund at the Boulder Community Foundation with earnings from *Into Thin Air*. As of 2012, the fund had donated more than $1.7 million to such charities as the American Himalayan Foundation, Educate the Children, Veterans Helping Veterans Now, the Access Fund, and the Boulder Valley Women's Health Center.

Krakauer's writing has been published by *Outside, GQ, National Geographic, Rolling Stone, Architectural Digest, Playboy, The New Yorker, The New York Times*, and Byliner.com. An article he wrote for Smithsonian about volcanology received the 1997 Walter Sullivan Award for Excellence in Science Journalism. His 1996 book, *Into the Wild*, remained on the New York Times bestseller list for more than two years.

Major Works
Eiger Dreams: Ventures Among Men and Mountains (1990)
Into the Wild (1996)
Into Thin Air (1997)
Under the Banner of Heaven: A Story of Violent Faith (2003)
Where Men Win Glory: The Odyssey of Pat Tillman (2009)
Three Cups of Deceit (2011)

INTRODUCTION *Into the Wild*

This LitPlan has been designed to develop students' reading, writing, thinking, and language skills through exercises and activities related to *Into the Wild*. It includes eighteen lessons, supported by extra resource materials.

The first lesson gives students an **introduction to the book** by having them brainstorm a list of things they would need to take with them to survive in the wilderness of Alaska for 100 days, with the constraint that whatever they choose has to fit in a backpack, able to be carried with the traveler.

The **reading assignments** are approximately thirty pages each; some are a little shorter, while others are a little longer. Students have approximately 15 minutes of pre-reading work to do prior to each reading assignment. This pre-reading work involves reviewing the study questions for the assignment and doing some vocabulary work for selected vocabulary words they will encounter in their reading.

The **study questions** are fact-based questions; students can find the answers to these questions right in the text. These questions come in two formats: short answer and multiple choice. The best use of these materials is probably to use the short answer version of the questions as study guides for students (since answers will be more complete), and to use the multiple choice version for occasional quizzes.

The **vocabulary** work is intended to enrich students' vocabularies as well as to aid in students' understanding of the book. Prior to each reading assignment, students will complete a two-part worksheet for selected vocabulary words in the upcoming reading assignment. Part I focuses on students' use of general knowledge and contextual clues by giving the sentence in which the word appears in the text and inviting students to write down what they think the words mean based on the usage in the sentences. Part II offers the definitions of the words in a matching format to help students clarify the word meanings.

After each reading assignment, students will formulate answers for the study questions. Discussion of these questions serves as a **review of the most important events and ideas** presented in the reading assignments. Teachers choose whether they want to have students formulate answers to the questions prior to the group discussion and choose the methods by which the material will be covered (small groups, whole class, individual work, game scenario, etc.).

After students complete the reading of the book, time is devoted to addressing **critical thinking**, higher-level questions (comparison/contrast, exploring character motivations, etc.), as well as discussing themes and other **elements of fiction**.

There is a **vocabulary review lesson**, which pulls together all of the fragmented vocabulary lists for the reading assignments and gives students a review of all the words they have studied. There is also a unit review lesson to bring together all elements of the unit and to help to prepare students for the final evaluation via the unit test.

There are three **writing assignments** in this unit, each with the purpose of informing, persuading, or having students express personal opinions. In the first writing assignment students write a letter from Gene Rosellini, John Mallon Waterman, Carl McCunn, or Everett Ruess to Jon Krakauer explaining why he attempted to survive alone in the wilderness. In the second writing assignment, students write a persuasive essay in which they defend their position that McCandless either was or was not suicidal. In the third writing assignment, students write a critical review of *Into the*

Wild for a newspaper book review column.

This unit plan includes a nonfiction **reading assignment**. Students must read nonfiction materials to gather information about assigned topics.

The **review lesson** pulls together all of the aspects of the unit. The teacher is given choices of activities or games to use, which all serve the same basic function of reviewing all of the information presented in the unit.

The **unit test** comes in two formats: multiple choice or short answer. As a convenience, two different tests for each format have been included. There is also an advanced short answer unit test for advanced students.

Additional support materials are included at the end of the unit. The **Unit Resource Materials** section includes a list of related topics for discussion or research, crossword and word search puzzles related to the book, and extra worksheets. There is a list of bulletin board ideas, and there is a list of additional activities the teacher could choose from to enhance the unit or as a substitution for an exercise the teacher may feel is inappropriate for his or her class. The **Vocabulary Resource Materials** section includes similar worksheets and games to reinforce the vocabulary words.

Answer keys are located directly after the reproducible student materials throughout the unit.

The **level** of this unit can be varied depending upon the criteria on which the individual assignments are graded, the teacher's expectations of his/her students in class discussions, and the formats chosen for the study guides, quizzes and test. If teachers have other activities they wish to use, they can usually easily be inserted prior to the review lesson.

Copyright Information: Reproduction of this publication is limited to one single-teacher, single-classroom license. Photocopying of this copyrighted product is permissible for one teacher for his or her own classroom use only. No part of this publication may be translated, stored in a retrieval system, or transmitted, distributed, posted, displayed or shared in any way or by any means (electronic, digital, mechanical, photocopying, recording, or otherwise) without prior written permission from Teacher's Pet Publications. Reproduction of any part of this publication for multiple school terms, an entire school or for a school system, by for-profit institutions and tutoring centers, or for commercial sale is strictly prohibited.

UNIT PLAN ADAPTATIONS

<u>Block Schedule</u>

Depending on the length of your class periods and the frequency with which the class meets, you may wish to choose one of the following options:
- Complete two of the daily lessons in one class period.
- Have students complete all reading and writing activities in class.
- Assign all reading to be completed out of class, and concentrate on the worksheets and discussions in class.
- Use some of the Unit and Vocabulary Resource activities during every class.

<u>Gifted & Talented / Advanced Classes</u>
- Emphasize the projects and the extra discussion questions.
- Have students complete all of the writing activities.
- Assign the reading to be completed out of class and focus on the discussions in class.
- Encourage students to develop their own questions.

<u>ESL / ELD</u>
- Assign a partner to help the student read the text aloud.
- Tape record the text and have the student listen and follow along in the text.
- Give the student the study guide worksheets to use as they read.
- Provide pictures and demonstrations to explain difficult vocabulary words and concepts.
- Create a summary of each chapter that includes the main points in a text that is written at a lower, more accessible reading level.

UNIT OBJECTIVES *Into the Wild*

1. Students will examine the elements of fiction as they apply to *Into the Wild*
2. Students will study the causes and effects of Chris McCandless's actions
3. Students will think critically to determine what items are necessary for survival
4. Students will find, read, and evaluate a nonfiction article about a young person who has attempted something as dangerous (some may say foolish) as Chris McCandless did.
5. Students will demonstrate their understanding of the text on four levels: factual, interpretive, critical, and personal.
6. Students will make connections with the material in the text and apply the lessons learned to their lives.
7. Students will answer questions to demonstrate their knowledge and understanding of the main events and characters as they relate to the author's theme development.
8. Students will enrich their vocabularies and improve their understanding of the book through the vocabulary lessons prepared for use in conjunction with the book.
9. Students will participate in large and small group discussions.
10. The writing assignments in this unit are designed for several purposes:
    a. to check and increase students' reading comprehension.
    b. to make students think about the ideas presented by the book.
    c. to encourage logical thinking.
    d. to provide an opportunity to practice good grammar and improve students' use of the English language.
    e. to encourage students' creativity.
    f. to practice writing to inform, to persuade, and to express personal opinions.

READING ASSIGNMENTS *Into the Wild*

Date Assigned	Assignment	Completion Date
	Part I: Author's Note The Alaska Interior The Stampede Trail	
	Part II: Carthage Detrital Wash Bullhead City Anza-Borrego Carthage	
	Part III: Alaska Davis Gulch Fairbanks	
	Part IV: Chesapeake Beach Annandale Virginia Beach	
	Part V: The Stikine Ice Cap The Stikine Ice Cap	
	Part VI: The Alaska Interior The Stampede Trail The Stampede Trail Epilogue	

UNIT OUTLINE *Into the Wild*

1 Introduction Activity PV for Part I	2 Read Part I	3 Review Part I PVR Part II	4 Review Part II Mapping First Person Encounters PV Part III	5 Writing Assignment #1 Read Part III
6 Quiz Part III Oral Presentations Nonfiction Research PV IV	7 Nonfiction Research	8 Review Part IV Research Presentations	9 PVR Part V Oral Reading Eval	10 Review Part V Writing #2 PV Part VI
11 Route Mapping Read VI Finish Oral Reading Eval	12 Review VI Role-Playing	13 Role-Playing Extra Discussion ?s	14 Extra Discussion ?s Writing #3	15 Vocabulary Review
16 Theme Review Quote Worksheet	17 Unit Review	18 Unit Test		

Key: P = Preview Study Questions   V = Vocabulary Work   R = Read

STUDY GUIDE QUESTIONS

SHORT ANSWER QUESTIONS *Into the Wild*

Part I
1. Identify Chris McCandless.
2. Identify Alexander Supertramp.
3. Identify Jim Gallien.
4. List Alex's gear and explain why Gallien believed it to be inadequate to survive the Alaskan wilderness.
5. How did Gallien try to dissuade Alex from carrying out his plan to live alone in the Alaskan wilderness?
6. Why did Alex ignore Gallien's warnings?
7. What gifts did Alex accept from Gallien? What did he give Gallien in return?
8. Why did Yutan Construction place three junked buses in the wilderness?
9. Identify the six people who visited bus 142 on September 6, 1992.
10. Aside from a decomposing body, what else was found in bus 142?

Part II
1. Identify Wayne Westerberg.
2. How did Westerberg try to help McCandless?
3. For what reasons did Westerberg describe McCandless as both ethical and intelligent?
4. Why did McCandless leave Carthage after only two weeks?
5. In what ways did McCandless demonstrate that he considered Westerberg a friend and Carthage his home?
6. Describe McCandless's middle-class family in Annandale, Virginia.
7. Why did Chris refuse to accept the new car his parents wanted to buy him as a graduation present from Emory University?
8. What did Chis do with the twenty-four thousand dollars in his savings account?
9. Why did Walt and Billie McCandless become very worried about their son in early August?
10. Why did McCandless abandon his beloved Datsun?
11. What other gear did McCandless abandon with the Datsun?
12. How did the Park Service rangers utilize McCandless's car?
13. Identify Jan Burres and describe her relationship with McCandless.
14. What did Walt and Billie learn from the private investigator they hired to find Chris?
15. Why did McCandless purchase an aluminum canoe?
16. Who helped McCandless finally reach the Gulf of California with his canoe?
17. McCandless stayed in Bullhead City, Arizona for two months. Where was he employed?
18. Identify Charlie. How did he help McCandless?
19. How did Charlie describe McCandless's character to the author?
20. Why did McCandless leave Bullhead City?

21. Describe the Slabs.
22. Identify Ron Franz.
23. How was the Salton Sea created?
24. What skill did Franz teach McCandless? What did McCandless make?
25. What special request did Ron Franz make that made McCandless uncomfortable?
26. What advice did McCandless give Franz in his letter? How did Franz respond to McCandless's words?
27. How did Franz respond when he heard about McCandless's death?

Part III
1. Why were many Alaskans critical of the author's article in *Outside* magazine?
2. Identify the Mayor of Hippie Cove.
3. List three ways John Waterman's life story parallels Chris McCandless's story.
4. List three ways John Waterman's life story differed from Chris McCandless's story.
5. What was Carl McCunn's big mistake?
6. Identify Everett Ruess.
7. Who was Lan Rameau?
8. In the opinion of Ken Sleight, how did Ruess die?
9. Why did the monks, known as *papar*, risk their lives to cross the ocean from Ireland to Iceland?
10. What was listed as the cause of McCandless's death in *The New York Times* article about the unknown young hiker found in the Alaskan wilderness?
11. How did Westerberg help the authorities locate McCandless's family?

Part IV
1. How long after Chris's body was discovered did the author interview Walt McCandless?
2. How did Chris's disappearance in 1990 change Walt McCandless?
3. Describe an event from Chris's high school physics class that illustrated his determination to follow his own path.
4. Identify Loren Johnson.
5. What damaged Chris's relationship with Carine?
6. Who was Buckley?
7. Identify Kris Maxie Gillmer.
8. List three social issues Chris felt passionate about in high school.
9. Why did Billie McCandless describe her son as "an entrepreneur"?
10. What did Chris do the summer before entering Emory University?
11. What advice did Walt give Chris after learning Chris was lost in the Mojave Desert? How did Chris react to his father's concern?
12. What did Chris do the summer between his freshman and sophomore years at Emory that helped his parents?

13. Despite his many skills, what surprising job did Chris take the summer between his sophomore and junior years at Emory?
14. What did Chris learn about Walt and Billie's past that greatly damaged his relationship with his father?
15. What trip did Chris take the summer between his junior and senior years at Emory?
16. How did Billie and Walt react to their son's death?

Part V
1. As a young man, what adventure did the author fantasize about undertaking?
2. What is the Devils Thumb? Why was the author drawn to it?
3. What assets did the author have with him when he departed Boulder to begin his journey to the Devils Thumb?
4. What was the purpose of the pair of aluminum curtain rods the author carried with him on his trek up thirty miles of glaciers to reach the base of the Devils Thumb?
5. How did the author transport enough food and gear to the Stikine Ice Cap to last for a three to four week stay?
6. How far did the author climb on the first day? Why did he abandon the climb?
7. What troubled the author the most about the fire in his tent?
8. Describe the blueprint for success the author's father drew for his children.
9. Why was the author's father admitted to a psychiatric hospital?
10. How many times did the author attempt to climb the Devils Thumb? Why was he successful on his last try?
11. What did the author do once he reached the summit of Devils Thumb?
12. How did the people of Kito's Kave bar react to the news that the author had successfully climbed the Devils Thumb?

Part VI
1. McCandless planned to hitchhike a thousand miles from Liard to Fairbanks. How far did Gaylord Stuckey drive McCandless?
2. What reasons did McCandless give Stuckey for his decision to spend the summer living off the land in the Alaskan bush?
3. What two requests did Stuckey make of McCandless when he dropped him off at the University of Alaska campus?
4. What was the heaviest item in McCandless's backpack?
5. Why did McCandless decide to make bus 142 his base camp?
6. What kinds of animals did McCandless kill for food?
7. How did McCandless try (unsuccessfully) to preserve the moose meat?
8. What was the first of "two pivotal setbacks" experienced by McCandless?
9. In the author's opinion, what small item did McCandless lack that may have saved his life?
10. Who accompanied the author on his journey to bus 142?

11. How did the author and his companions cross the Teklanika River?
12. What did the author first see when he entered bus 142?
13. What was the subject of most of McCandless's journal entries?
14. What was the last book McCandless read?
15. Why did McCandless begin to eat the seeds rather than the roots of the wild potato?
16. What food, in the author's opinion, caused McCandless to starve to death?
17. What significant milestone did McCandless note in his journal even though he was weak and starving?
18. Why did the authorities conclude that McCandless did not vandalize the nearby cabins?
19. McCandless might have been rescued if he had started a forest fire as a distress signal. Why, in his sister Carine's opinion, did McCandless fail to do this?
20. What evidence did McCandless leave behind showing that he was happy before he died?
21. After visiting the site of their son's death, what did Billie and Walt leave behind in bus 142?

SHORT ANSWER QUESTIONS ANSWER KEY *Into the Wild*

Part I

1. Identify Chris McCandless.
   Chris McCandless, raised in a suburb of Washington, D.C., was a recent graduate of Emory University located in Atlanta, Georgia. He was an excellent student from an affluent family. In 1990, McCandless changed his name, gave away his entire twenty-four-thousand dollars of savings, and cut off contact with his family to travel alone across the country. McCandless eventually died of starvation in the Alaskan wilderness.

2. Identify Alexander Supertramp.
   Alexander Supertramp was the name Chris McCandless selected for himself.

3. Identify Jim Gallien.
   Jim Gallien was an electrician traveling to Anchorage. He gave Alex a ride to the Denali National Park.

4. List Alex's gear and explain why Gallien believed it to be inadequate to survive the Alaskan wilderness.
   The only food Alex was carrying was a ten-pound bag of rice. His .22 caliber rifle was too small to kill large game. Alex's hiking boots were not waterproof. He had no ax, no snowshoes, and no bug dope. Alex had a road map, but no compass. Alex also had a small camera in his backpack. Gallien used this camera to snap a photo of Alex.

5. How did Gallien try to dissuade Alex from carrying out his plan to live alone in the Alaskan wilderness?
   Gallien warned Alex that hunting was not easy. He tried to scare Alex with bear stories and pointed out that Alex's gun was no defense against a bear. He offered to drive Alex to Anchorage and buy him decent gear.

6. Why did Alex ignore Gallien's warnings?
   Alex was confident in his ability to handle any situations that might arise.

7. What gifts did Alex accept from Gallien? What did he give Gallien in return?
   Alex accepted a pair of rubber work boots, two grilled-cheese-and-tuna sandwiches, and a bag of corn chips. Alex gave Gallien eighty-five cents in change, his watch, and his comb.

8. Why did Yutan Construction place three junked buses in the wilderness?
   In 1961, Yutan Construction Company upgraded the Stampede Trail. The buses, outfitted with bunks and a stove, were placed in the wilderness to serve as housing for construction workers.

9. Identify the six people who visited bus 142 on September 6, 1992.
   Ken Thompson (the owner of an Anchorage auto-body shop), Gordon Samel (his employee), and Ferdie Swanson (a construction worker) were in the wilderness hunting moose when they visited bus 142. There, they met an unnamed boy and girl from Anchorage who were near the bus but afraid to enter due to the bad smell. The last person to arrive was Butch Killian; a hunter from Healy who alerted the troopers that there was a body in bus 142.

10. Aside from a decomposing body, what else was found in bus 142?
    The author notes that a red signal flag made from a leg warmer, a handwritten note, a Remington rifle, a box of shells, paperback books, jeans, cooking gear, a backpack, a sleeping bag, a camera with five rolls of film, and a field guide to edible plants that was also used as a diary were found with McCandless's remains.

Part II

1. Identify Wayne Westerberg.
   Westerberg owned grain elevators in Carthage, South Dakota. He had thick shoulders and a black goatee.

2. How did Westerberg try to help McCandless?
   Westerberg gave McCandless a place to stay for three days and offered him a job should McCandless return to Carthage one day.

3. For what reasons did Westerberg describe McCandless as both ethical and intelligent?
   Westerberg described McCandless as ethical because he never quit in the middle of a job. Westerberg considered McCandless intelligent because McCandless read a lot, used big words, and thought deeply trying "to make sense of the world."

4. Why did McCandless leave Carthage after only two weeks?
   Westerberg was arrested and sentenced to four months in jail for selling illegal equipment designed to unscramble cable signals. With his friend Westerberg in jail, McCandless had no job, so he left Carthage.

5. In what ways did McCandless demonstrate that he considered Westerberg a friend and Carthage his home?
   When McCandless left Carthage, he gave Westerberg a copy of Tolstoy's War and Peace. *He regularly wrote or called Westerberg and had his mail forwarded to Westerberg. McCandless told new acquaintances he met on the road that Carthage, South Dakota was his home.*

6. Describe McCandless's middle-class family in Annandale, Virginia.
   Walt McCandless was an aerospace engineer who worked for NASA and Hughes Aircraft before beginning his own business with his wife and Chris' mother, Billie. Chris was close to his younger sister, Carine. In addition to Carine, Chris had six half-brothers and sisters from his father's first marriage.

7. Why did Chris refuse to accept the new car his parents wanted to buy him as a graduation present from Emory University?
   Chris did not want to accept gifts from his parents because he believed gifts were their way of buying his respect.

8. What did Chis do with the twenty-four thousand dollars in his savings account?
   Chris donated the money to OXFAM America, which was a nonprofit organization formed to fight hunger.

9. Why did Walt and Billie McCandless become very worried about their son in early August?
   Walt and Billie traveled to Atlanta to visit Chris in early August because they had not heard from him all summer. They discovered Chris long gone and his room empty. Disappointed, they returned home to find that Chris had arranged for his mail to be held in Atlanta until August first and then transferred to his home address. He deliberately did this to prevent his family from learning that he was on the road until it was too late for them to interfere with his plans.

10. Why did McCandless abandon his beloved Datsun?
    The Datsun was damaged in a flash flood. McCandless drained the battery trying to get it started, so he wrote a note giving the car to anyone who was capable of getting the car out of the backcountry.

11. What other gear did McCandless abandon with the Datsun?
    McCandless left behind his car, a Gianini guitar, a saucepan with $4.93 in change, a football, a bag of old clothes, a fishing rod and tackle, an electric razor, a harmonica, jumper cables, twenty-five pounds of rice, and his car keys.

12. How did the Park Service rangers utilize McCandless's car?
    The Park Service used McCandless's Datsun as an undercover vehicle to make drug-related arrests.

13. Identify Jan Burres and describe her relationship with McCandless.
    Jan Burres and her boyfriend Bob were drifters who made a living by selling knick-knacks at flea markets. They found McCandless on the side of the road picking berries and offered him food and a ride. McCandless reminded Jan of her son who left years earlier. McCandless stayed with them for a couple of weeks.

14. What did Walt and Billie learn from the private investigator they hired to find Chris?
    The McCandlesses learned that their son gave his twenty-four thousand dollars of savings to charity.

15. Why did McCandless purchase an aluminum canoe?
    McCandless decided to use the canoe to travel down the Colorado River to the Gulf of California.

16. Who helped McCandless finally reach the Gulf of California with his canoe?
    Unable to find a passable waterway to the Gulf of California, McCandless accepted a ride from some duck hunters.

17. McCandless stayed in Bullhead City, Arizona for two months. Where was he employed?
    McCandless worked at McDonald's.

18. Identify Charlie. How did he help McCandless?
    Charlie was an old man who encountered McCandless in a public restroom. When he learned that McCandless was homeless and camping in the open, he offered McCandless the use of an old trailer.

19. How did Charlie describe McCandless's character to the author?
    Charlie described McCandless as moody and temperamental. He remembered that McCandless read a lot of books, especially Jack London books, about Alaska. He believed that McCandless did not like to be around people and that he seemed to be looking for something. Charlie thought McCandless was a nice guy with a lot of "complexes."

20. Why did McCandless leave Bullhead City?
    McCandless left Bullhead City because he was "tired of punching a clock, tired of the 'plastic people' he worked with, and decided to get the hell out of town."

21. Describe the Slabs.
    The Slabs was an old navy air base located three miles outside of Niland, California. The base was leveled, leaving only the concrete slabs where buildings once stood. Many vagabonds settled in the Slabs in warm California to escape the cold winters elsewhere.

22. Identify Ron Franz.
    Ron Franz was an eighty-year-old man who met McCandless in January 1992. He gave McCandless a ride to his camp located a half mile past Oh-My-God Hot Springs near Salton City, California. To fill the void in his life created when his wife and son were killed by a drunk driver in 1957, Franz "adopted" needy young Okinawan boys and girls.

23. How was the Salton Sea created?
    The Salton Sea was a small ocean created in 1905 from an engineering mistake. The plan was to dig a canal from the Colorado River to irrigate farmland in the Imperial Valley. Overflow from the river traveled into the newly dug canal and into the Salton sink. The water covered four hundred miles of desert.

24. What skill did Franz teach McCandless? What did McCandless make?
    Franz taught McCandless the secrets of leatherworking. McCandless made a leather belt with a pictorial record of his adventures.

25. What special request did Ron Franz make that made McCandless uncomfortable?
    Franz asked McCandless if he could adopt him.
26. What advice did McCandless give Franz in his letter? How did Franz respond to McCandless's words?
    McCandless advised Franz to leave Salton City and to lead a nomadic life. In this way, McCandless believed Franz would be able to see and appreciate "all of the wonderful things that God has placed around us to discover." Franz listened to McCandless's advice. He sold most of his possessions, bought a GMC Duravan, and went to live on the bajada.
27. How did Franz respond when he heard about McCandless's death?
    Franz became an atheist.

Part III
1. Why were many Alaskans critical of the author's article in *Outside* magazine?
   Many critics believed McCandless was a "greenhorn" and a "kook" who went unprepared into the Alaskan wilderness. They thought he was undeserving of the attention Krakauer gave him in the article.
2. Identify the Mayor of Hippie Cove.
   Gene Rosellini was about forty years old. He had a bushy black beard and long hair. As a young man he left a promising academic career to live a squatter-like existence at Hippie Cove. He was attempting to live the life of a Stone Age native. Rosellini died after attempting to walk around the world with only the supplies he could carry in his backpack.
3. List three ways John Waterman's life story parallels Chris McCandless's story.
   Both young men were raised in the Washington D.C. area. In addition, they both had poor relationships with their fathers. Waterman and McCandless both embarked on risky adventures knowing that they may never return.
4. List three ways John Waterman's life story differed from Chris McCandless's story.
   Waterman spent time in a mental hospital. McCandless often lived on the fringes of society, but was never diagnosed with a mental disorder. Waterman maintained a complete written record of his adventures. McCandless wrote sporadically about his life. Waterman was well regarded as an expert mountaineer before his fatal climb. McCandless was perceived by many Alaskans as a "greenhorn" who was unprepared to survive alone in the Alaskan wilderness.
5. What was Carl McCunn's big mistake?
   When a rescue plane flew over his campsite, McCunn mistakenly used the wrong emergency hand signal. Instead of communicating to the pilot that he needed to be rescued, McCunn gave the wrong signal that communicated to the pilot that he was fine and did not need to be rescued.
6. Identify Everett Ruess.
   Everett Ruess was born in 1914. His family moved frequently until settling in southern California. Ruess attended high school and art school. Beginning at the age of sixteen, Ruess began solo journeys hitchhiking and stopping at remote western settlements. At the age of twenty, he vanished.
7. Who was Lan Rameau?
   Lan Rameau was Everett Ruess's alias.
8. In the opinion of Ken Sleight, how did Ruess die?
   Sleight believed Ruess drowned trying to cross the Colorado River.

9. Why did the monks, known as *papar*, risk their lives to cross the ocean from Ireland to Iceland?
   The monks were searching for "lonely places" away from civilization where they could dwell free of the "temptations of the world."
10. What was listed as the cause of McCandless's death in *The New York Times* article about the unknown young hiker found in the Alaskan wilderness?
    The cause of death was listed as starvation.
11. How did Westerberg help the authorities locate McCandless's family?
    Westerberg heard a Paul Harvey radio broadcast about the unknown hiker. Westerberg believed the hiker could be Chris, so he phoned the Alaska State Troopers. Westerberg had McCandless's correct social security number from a W-4 form McCandless completed when he worked for Westerberg. With this information, the authorities located Chris's half-brother, Sam.

Part IV
1. How long after Chris's body was discovered did the author interview Walt McCandless?
   The interview took place seven weeks later.
2. How did Chris's disappearance in 1990 change Walt McCandless?
   His volatile temper subsided. He became a more tolerant man.
3. Describe an event from Chris's high school physics class that illustrated his determination to follow his own path.
   Chris received a failing grade on his lab reports, even though he correctly completed the work, because he refused to write the reports in the teacher's prescribed format.
4. Identify Loren Johnson.
   Loren Johnson was Chris's adored grandfather who had an "affinity for the wilderness."
5. What damaged Chris's relationship with Carine?
   Their relationship was damaged by a musical rivalry. Although both Chris and Carine were talented musicians, Carine was a better French horn player.
6. Who was Buckley?
   Buckley was the family dog.
7. Identify Kris Maxie Gillmer.
   Gillmer was Chris's closest friend in high school.
8. List three social issues Chris felt passionate about in high school.
   McCandless felt passionate about race issues, including apartheid in South Africa, the plight of the homeless, and the need to eliminate hunger in this country.
9. Why did Billie McCandless describe her son as "an entrepreneur"?
   Chris excelled at making money. At age eight, he successfully sold vegetables to the neighbors. He ran his own copy business at age twelve. In high school, Chris was a top door-to-door salesman for a local contractor.
10. What did Chris do the summer before entering Emory University?
    Chris drove across the country in his Datsun.
11. What advice did Walt give Chris after learning Chris was lost in the Mojave Desert? How did Chris react to his father's concern?
    Walt suggested that Chris should be careful and let his parents know his whereabouts. Chris was angered by this advice. He thought his parents were idiots to worry about him.

12. What did Chris do the summer between his freshman and sophomore years at Emory that helped his parents?
    Chris worked at his parents' business writing computer software.
13. Despite his many skills, what surprising job did Chris take the summer between his sophomore and junior years at Emory?
    Chris delivered pizzas.
14. What did Chris learn about Walt and Billie's past that greatly damaged his relationship with his father?
    Chris learned that his father did not make a clean break with his first wife. He fathered a son with his first wife after he fell in love with Billie and fathered Chris.
15. What trip did Chris take the summer between his junior and senior years at Emory?
    Chris drove to Alaska.
16. How did Billie and Walt react to their son's death?
    Billie lost weight but Walt gained eight pounds. Billie collected pictures of Chris's life and wept over them. The author described Billie's grief as "a sense of loss so huge and irreparable that the mind balks at taking its measure."

Part V

1. As a young man, what adventure did the author fantasize about undertaking?
   The author fantasized about conquering remote ascents of various mountains in Alaska and Canada.
2. What is the Devils Thumb? Why was the author drawn to it?
   The Devils Thumb is a Colorado mountain with a spectacular, glacier-sculpted peak. The north wall of Devils Thumb had never been conquered, so this mountain was especially interesting to the author.
3. What assets did the author have with him when he departed Boulder to begin his journey to the Devils Thumb?
   He had a 1960 Pontiac Star Chief and two hundred dollars.
4. What was the purpose of the pair of aluminum curtain rods the author carried with him on his trek up thirty miles of glaciers to reach the base of the Devils Thumb?
   The author tied the rods together to form a cross. He then strapped the cross to his backpack so that the rods extended away from his body. He hoped the curtain rods would span the width of any hidden crevasses he might accidentally uncover and prevent him from slipping into the unknown depths of the glacier ice.
5. How did the author transport enough food and gear to the Stikine Ice Cap to last for a three to four week stay?
   The author paid a pilot $150.00 to drop six cartons of supplies at the base of the Devils Thumb.
6. How far did the author climb on the first day? Why did he abandon the climb?
   The author climbed almost seven hundred feet when the frost feathers became too thin to continue.
7. What troubled the author the most about the fire in his tent?
   The author borrowed the expensive tent from his father. He worried that by destroying the tent, he had, once again, lived up to his father's worst expectations.
8. Describe the blueprint for success the author's father drew for his children.
   He wanted his children to excel in all areas of school, go to the "right" college, and ultimately attend Harvard Medical School.

9. Why was the author's father admitted to a psychiatric hospital?
   The author's father, a physician, suffered from a painful condition called post-polio syndrome. He attempted to use medications to stop the decline in his motor skills. The heavy use of these medications led to delusional behavior. After a suicide attempt, the author's father was placed in a psychiatric hospital.
10. How many times did the author attempt to climb the Devils Thumb? Why was he successful on his last try?
    The author attempted to climb the Devils Thumb three times. He was successful on his third try because he changed his route from the north side of the Devils Thumb to the less dangerous southeast face.
11. What did the author do once he reached the summit of Devils Thumb?
    He took pictures to prove he was successful.
12. How did the people of Kito's Kave bar react to the news that the author had successfully climbed the Devils Thumb?
    They were not surprised or impressed. Mostly, they did not care.

Part VI
1. McCandless planned to hitchhike a thousand miles from Liard to Fairbanks. How far did Gaylord Stuckey drive McCandless?
   Stuckey drove McCandless all of the way to Fairbanks.
2. What reasons did McCandless give Stuckey for his decision to spend the summer living off the land in the Alaskan bush?
   McCandless wanted to prove to himself that he could survive without any help.
3. What two requests did Stuckey make of McCandless when he dropped him off at the University of Alaska campus?
   Stuckey asked McCandless to send him a letter when he returned from the wild, and he pleaded with McCandless to call his parents.
4. What was the heaviest item in McCandless's backpack?
   McCandless carried nine or ten paperback books.
5. Why did McCandless decide to make bus 142 his base camp?
   He concluded that the area around the bus was sufficiently isolated from civilization to meet his needs.
6. What kinds of animals did McCandless kill for food?
   McCandless killed ducks, squirrels, porcupines, birds, a Canada goose, and a moose.
7. How did McCandless try (unsuccessfully) to preserve the moose meat?
   McCandless tried to smoke the meat.
8. What was the first of "two pivotal setbacks" experienced by McCandless?
   On July 3rd, McCandless decided to leave the bush, but found that he could not safely cross the swollen Teklanika River due to the summer snowmelt from the glaciers.
9. In the author's opinion, what small item did McCandless lack that may have saved his life?
   McCandless lacked a good topographic map of the area.
10. Who accompanied the author on his journey to bus 142?
    The author traveled with Roman Dial, Dan Solie, and Andrew Liske.

11. How did the author and his companions cross the Teklanika River?
    They walked a half-mile to an abandoned gauging station where they found a cable spanning the river. Using an aluminum basket suspended from the cable and a system of pulleys, they pulled themselves across.

12. What did the author first see when he entered bus 142?
    The author saw the mattress where McCandless died.

13. What was the subject of most of McCandless's journal entries?
    McCandless wrote about food more than anything else.

14. What was the last book McCandless read?
    The last book McCandless read was Doctor Zhivago.

15. Why did McCandless begin to eat the seeds rather than the roots of the wild potato?
    In the summer, the roots of the wild potato became too tough to eat.

16. What food, in the author's opinion, caused McCandless to starve to death?
    In the author's opinion, McCandless died of swainsonine poisoning caused by eating moldy wild potato seeds.

17. What significant milestone did McCandless note in his journal even though he was weak and starving?
    McCandless noted in his journal that he had survived 100 days in the bush.

18. Why did the authorities conclude that McCandless did not vandalize the nearby cabins?
    There was no evidence in McCandless's journal or in his photographs to indicate that he knew about the cabins.

19. McCandless might have been rescued if he had started a forest fire as a distress signal. Why, in his sister Carine's opinion, did McCandless fail to do this?
    Carine believed that her brother would never burn a forest, even to save his own life.

20. What evidence did McCandless leave behind showing that he was happy before he died?
    McCandless took a photograph of himself standing outside the bus, smiling, and holding his last note. "I HAVE HAD A HAPPY LIFE AND THANK THE LORD. GOODBYE AND MAY GOD BLESS ALL!"

21. After visiting the site of their son's death, what did Billie and Walt leave behind in bus 142?
    They left a small brass plaque, wild flowers, and an emergency kit with a note instructing anyone who found the bus to call his or her parents.

MULTIPLE CHOICE QUESTIONS *Into the Wild*

Part I

1. Which of the following is NOT true about Chris McCandless?
    A. Chris was a recent graduate of Emory University, located in Atlanta, Georgia.
    B. Chris was an excellent student from an affluent family.
    C. Chris gave away his entire twenty-four thousand dollar savings.
    D. Chris admired his parents, especially his father, and kept in touch with them throughout his journeys.

2. Identify Alexander Supertramp.
    A. Alexander Supertramp was the name Chris McCandless selected for himself.
    B. Alexander Supertramp was a young man who went into the Alaskan wilderness a couple of years before McCandless. He did not survive.
    C. Alexander Supertramp was a character in one of McCandless's books. McCandless was trying to retrace Alex's journey.
    D. Alexander Supertramp was McCandless's father's derogatory name for Chris.

3. Identify Jim Gallien.
    A. Jim Gallien gave Alex a ride to the Denali National Park.
    B. Jim Gallien hired Alex to work in his restaurant.
    C. Jim Gallien told Alex where to find the bus for shelter.
    D. Jim Gallien bought Alex new gear.

4. Which of the statements below is NOT one Gallien used to explain to Alex why his gear was inadequate to survive the Alaskan wilderness?
    A. Alex's .22 caliber rifle was too small to kill large game.
    B. Alex had a road map but no compass.
    C. Alex's supply of dried salmon was insufficient for an extended stay in the bush.
    D. Alex's hiking boots were not waterproof.

5. Which of the following is NOT one way Gallien tried to dissuade Alex from carrying out his plan to live in the Alaskan wilderness?
    A. Gallien warned Alex that the weather in Alaska can change very quickly, stranding unsuspecting people in blizzard conditions.
    B. Gallien warned Alex that hunting was not easy.
    C. Gallien tried to scare Alex with bear stories and pointed out that Alex's gun was no defense against a bear.
    D. Gallien warned Alex that his gear was not sufficient for survival in Alaska.

Multiple Choice Questions Part I *Into the Wild* Page 2

6. Jim Gallien tried to convince Alex to abandon his plans to spend the summer alone in the Alaskan bush. Why was he unsuccessful?
   A. Alex thought Gallien was overprotective, overcautious, and perhaps a bit jealous of his freedom and adventures.
   B. Alex thought Gallien was just trying to scare him into going home to his family.
   C. Alex was confident in his ability to handle any situations that might arise.
   D. Alex was suicidal and never planned to return from the bush. It didn't matter that he was unprepared.

7. What gifts did Alex accept from Gallien? What did he give Gallien in return?
   A. Alex accepted a bus ticket to Seattle. Alex gave Gallien $2.05, all the money he had in his pockets.
   B. Alex accepted rubber work boots and food. Alex gave Gallien eighty-five cents, his watch, and his comb.
   C. Alex accepted hiking boots and food. Alex gave Gallien the keys to his car.
   D. Alex accepted a guide to survival in Alaska. Alex gave Gallien his camera.

8. Why did Yutan Construction place three junked buses in the wilderness?
   A. The buses were to serve as navigation points.
   B. The buses were to serve as wildlife habitats.
   C. The buses were to serve as housing for construction workers.
   D. The buses were to serve as hunting lodges for local hunters.

9. Which of these people did NOT visit bus 142 on September 6, 1992?
   A. Wayne Westerberg
   B. Ken Thompson
   C. Butch Killian
   D. Gordon Samuel

10. Which of these things was NOT found in bus 142 when Chris's body was found?
    A. a Remington rifle
    B. a lantern
    C. paperback books
    D. a handwritten note

Part II

1. Identify Wayne Westerberg.
   A. Westerberg showed McCandless how to tool leather.
   B. Westerberg owned grain elevators in South Dakota.
   C. Westerberg and his wife traveled from place to place selling knick-knacks.
   D. Westerberg owned a lumber mill in North Dakota.

2. How did Westerberg try to help McCandless?
   A. Westerberg let McCandless use an old trailer that was next door to his, knowing the owners would not be back for several months.
   B. Westerberg gave McCandless rubber boots and some food.
   C. Westerberg bought McCandless dinner and gave him some money.
   D. Westerberg gave McCandless a place to stay for three days and offered him a job.

3. Which of the following statemtents is NOT something Westerberg said about McCandless?
   A. McCandless thought deeply trying to make sense of the world.
   B. McCandless was suicidal.
   C. McCandless was ethical because he never quit in the middle of a job.
   D. McCandless was intelligent because he read a lot.

4. Why did McCandless leave Carthage after only two weeks?
   A. McCandless was tired of the plastic people he worked with.
   B. McCandless wasn't making enough money.
   C. McCandless did not have a job after Westerberg went to jail.
   D. McCandless was about to be arrested for illegally rigging cable boxes.

5. Which of the following is NOT a way McCandless demonstrated that he considered Westerberg a friend and Carthage his home?
   A. McCandless regularly wrote or called Westerberg and had his mail forwarded to Carthage.
   B. McCandless told new acquaintances he met on the road that Carthage, South Dakota was his home.
   C. McCandless gave Westerberg a copy of Tolstoy's *War and Peace*.
   D. McCandless stayed with Westerberg and worked for him for almost a whole year.

6. Identify Walt, Billie, and Carine.
    A. Walt was Chris's father. Billie was Chris's mother. Carine was Chris's sister.
    B. Walt and Billie owned a grain elevator, where Chris worked. Carine was Chris's sister.
    C. Walt and Billie traveled around selling items at flea markets. Carine was their daughter.
    D. Walt, Billie, and Carine were the people who found Chris's body in the bus.

7. Why did Chris refuse to accept the new car his parents wanted to buy him as a graduation present from Emory University?
    A. Chris preferred to walk.
    B. Chris knew his parents needed the money themselves; he didn't want to take something so expensive from them when he knew they couldn't afford it.
    C. Chris liked his Datsun and did not want to give it up.
    D. Chris did not want to accept gifts from his parents because he believed gifts were their way of buying his respect.

8. What did Chis do with the twenty-four thousand dollars in his savings account?
    A. Chris donated the money to the Sierra Club.
    B. Chris donated the money to a nonprofit organization formed to fight hunger.
    C. Chris donated the money to Emory University.
    D. Chirs donated the money to an anti-apartheid group in South Africa.

9. Why did Walt and Billie McCandless become very worried about their son in early August?
    A. They knew Chris was on the road, but they hadn't heard from him all summer.
    B. They became concerned when Carine told them of Chris's plans in August.
    C. They went to Atlanta to visit him and discovered his apartment was empty; they had no idea where he had gone.
    D. They knew the school year was about to begin, but Chris had not yet returned from his cross-country trip.

10. Why did McCandless abandon his beloved Datsun?
    A. The Datsun was damaged in a flash flood. It wouldn't start, so he left it.
    B. He decided that by hiking he could live more naturally.
    C. McCandless had begun to view the car as part of the world's trappings of which he wanted to be free.
    D. Chris knew it would be of little use to him in the Alaskan wilderness.

Multiple Choice Questions Part II *Into the Wild* Page 3

11. Which of the following did McCandless NOT leave with the Datsun?
    A. rice
    B. a guitar
    C. a fishing rod and tackle
    D. a compass

12. How did the Park Service utilize McCandless's car?
    A. The Park Service used McCandless's Datsun as a training vehicle for park rangers.
    B. The Park Service used McCandless's Datsun as a storage container for emergency supplies.
    C. The Park Service used McCandless's Datsun as an undercover vehicle to make drug-related arrests.
    D. The Park Service used McCandless's Datsun as a shelter for travelers.

13. Which of the following statements is NOT true about Jan Burres and her relationship with McCandless?
    A. Jan Burres and her boyfriend found McCandless on the side of the road picking berries. They offered him food and a ride.
    B. Jan Burres and her boyfriend Bob were drifters who sold knick-knacks at flea markets.
    C. McCandless reminded Jan of her son who left years earlier.
    D. McCandless stayed with Jan Burres for five months.

14. What did Walt and Billie learn from the private investigator they hired to find Chris?
    A. They learned that their son was working at a grain elevator in South Dakota.
    B. They learned that their son had a car accident in the Arizona desert.
    C. They learned that their son died in Alaska.
    D. They learned that their son gave his savings to charity.

15. Why did McCandless purchase an aluminum canoe?
    A. He needed a way to haul his gear over the snow, ice, and rivers in Alaska.
    B. He needed a way to travel down the Teklanika River.
    C. He needed a way to travel down the Colorado River to the Gulf of California.
    D. He needed a way to get up the Sushana River.

16. Who helped McCandless finally reach the Gulf of California?
    A. Ron Franz
    B. Wayne Westerbrook
    C. moose hunters
    D. duck hunters

17. McCandless stayed in Bullhead City, Arizona for two months. Where was he employed?
    A. McCandless worked at a lumber yard.
    B. McCandless worked at a tannery.
    C. McCandless worked at McDonald's.
    D. McCandless worked at a ranch.

18. How did Charlie help McCandless?
    A. Charlie hired McCandless to help McCandless acquire enough money to continue on his journey.
    B. Charlie offered McCandless the use of an old trailer to live in.
    C. Charlie gave McCandless several books, including one about identifying edible plants in the wilderness of Alaska.
    D. Charlie gave McCandless a pair of rubber work boots.

19. Which of the following is NOT something Charlie said to describe McCandless's character to the author?
    A. Charlie described McCandless as temperamental.
    B. Charlie said McCandless seemed suicidal.
    C. Charlie described McCandless as moody.
    D. Charlie said McCandless did not like to be around people.

20. Why did McCandless leave Bullhead City?
    A. McCandless left Bullhead City because he needed to get on his way to Alaska, to arrive there just after the spring thaw.
    B. McCandless left Bullhead City because his employer was about to notify the authorities as to his whereabouts.
    C. McCandless left Bullhead City because he was tired of punching a clock and tired of the people he worked with.
    D. McCandless left Bullhead City because he got fired from his job.

21. Identify "the Slabs."
    A. "The Slabs" were what locals in the Alaskan wilderness called glaciers on the mountains.
    B. "The Slabs" were sheets of ice in the flatlands of the Alaskan wilderness. They were a welcome sight to McCandless as he emerged from the dense brush.
    C. "The Slabs" were the remains of a naval air base that had been leveled, where vagabonds gathered.
    D. "The Slabs" were a group of migrant workers in California. McCandless joined them briefly as he made his way northward towards Alaska.

22. Which of the following is NOT true about Ron Franz?
    A. Ron Franz's wife and son were killed by a drunk driver.
    B. Ron Franz adopted needy young Okinawan boys and girls.
    C. Ron Franz gave McCandless a ride to his camp near Salton City.
    D. Ron Franz was an outdoorsman and explorer who died trying to climb the Devils Thumb.

23. How was the Salton Sea created?
    A. It was created by an engineering mistake.
    B. It was created by a volcano.
    C. It was created by an asteroid.
    D. It was created by glaciers.

24. What skill did Franz teach McCandless? What did McCandless make?
    A. Franz taught McCandless leatherworking. McCandless made a leather belt.
    B. Franz taught McCandless how to skin animals. McCandless made a warm coat from the skins.
    C. Franz taught McCandless how to weld. McCandless made traps he would later use to catch small game in Alaska.
    D. Franz taught McCandless the proper way to smoke salmon. McCandless made twenty pounds of smoked salmon to take with him into the wildnerness.

25. What special request did Ron Franz make that made McCandless uncomfortable?
    A. Franz asked McCandless if he could adopt him.
    B. Franz asked McCandless if he could accompany him on the rest of his journey.
    C. Franz asked McCandless to date his daughter.
    D. Franz asked McCandless if he could notify his parents as to his whereabouts.

26. What advice did McCandless give Franz in his letter?
    A. McCandless advised Franz to find a good woman and get married.
    B. McCandless advised Franz to leave Salton City and lead a nomadic life.
    C. McCandless advised Franz to stop tampering with illegal cable boxes.
    D. McCandless advised Franz to remain in Salton City.

27. How did Franz respond when he heard about McCandless's death?
    A. Franz committed suicide.
    B. Franz became an atheist.
    C. Franz found religion.
    D. Franz traveled to see bus 142 where Chris died.

Part III

1. Why were many Alaskans critical of the author's article in *Outside* magazine?

    A. Many critics believed that Krakauer did not investigate the story thoroughly enough before it was published in the magazine.

    B. Many critics were afraid that the article would encourage a rush of more "kooks" to come to Alaska to try to live in the wild. They thought encouraging such a thing was irresponsible.

    C. Many critics believed McCandless was a "greenhorn" and a "kook" who went unprepared into the Alaskan wilderness. They thought he was undeserving of the attention Krakauer gave him in the article.

    D. Many critics thought the author was sensationalizing the McCandless story for his own gain, taking advantage of the unfortunate boy's situation.

2. Which of the following statements is NOT true about Gene Rosellini, the Mayor of Hippie Cove?

    A. Rosellini died after attempting to walk around the world with only the supplies he could carry in his backpack.

    B. Rosellini was attempting to live the life of a Stone Age man.

    C. Rosellini left a promising academic career to live a squatter-like existence at Hippie Cove.

    D. Rosellini came from an impoverished background and learned survival skills as a way of life as a young boy.

3. Which of the following is NOT a way John Waterman's life story parallels Chris McCandless's story.

    A. Waterman and McCandless both had mental disorders.

    B. Waterman and McCandless both embarked on risky adventures knowing that they may never return.

    C. Waterman and McCandless both had poor relationships with their fathers.

    D. Waterman and McCandless were both raised in the suburbs of Washington, D.C.

4. Which of the following is NOT a way John Waterman's life story differed from Chris McCandless's story.

    A. Waterman grew up in Alaska. McCandless grew up in the suburbs of Washington, D.C.

    B. Waterman was well regarded as an expert mountaineer before his fatal climb. McCandless was perceived by many Alaskans as a "greenhorn" who was unprepared to survive alone in the Alaskan wilderness.

    C. Waterman maintained a complete, written record of his adventures. McCandless wrote sporadically about his life.

    D. Waterman spent time in a mental hospital. McCandless often lived on the fringes of society, but he was never diagnosed with a mental disorder.

5. What was Carl McCunn's big mistake?
   A. McCunn miscalculated the thickness of the ice pack and fell through into the icy water.
   B. McCunn packed way too much film and not nearly enough supplies.
   C. McCunn attempted to cross the river when the water was too high. His belongings were swept away leaving him no radio to contact the plane that was to pick him up.
   D. McCunn failed to arrange for someone to pick him up from the island at the end of the summer.

6. Which of the following statements is NOT true about Everett Ruess?
   A. At the age of twenty Everett Ruess vanished.
   B. Everett Ruess's family moved frequently until settling in southern California.
   C. Beginning at the age of sixteen, Ruess began solo journeys by hitchhiking.
   D. McCandless read Ruess's journal, which gave him the idea of making his own solo journeys.

7. Who was Lan Rameau?
   A. Lan Rameau gave McCandless a ride to Denali National Park.
   B. Lan Rameau was Everett Ruess's alias.
   C. Lan Rameau was an outdoor adventurer who had also scribbled his name on the walls of bus 142.
   D. Lan Rameau was McCandless's half-brother.

8. In the opinion of Ken Sleight, how did Ruess die?
   A. Sleight believed Ruess drowned trying to cross the Colorado River.
   B. Sleight believed Ruess died of starvation.
   C. Sleight believed Reuss was mugged and murdered.
   D. Sleight believed Ruess was attacked and eaten by a bear.

9. Why did the monks, known as *papar*, risk their lives to cross the ocean from Ireland to Iceland?
   A. The monks were searching for places away from civilization where they could dwell free from the temptations of the world.
   B. The monks knew there were people in Iceland who desperately wanted to come to Ireland, so the monks risked their lives to rescue them.
   C. The monks were persecuted in Ireland and fled to Iceland where they knew they could live in peace.
   D. The monks believed they were being sent to Iceland on a mission from God. They weren't sure of the exact purpose of their mission, but they were drawn to go there.

10. What was listed as the cause of McCandless's death in *The New York Times* article about the unknown young hiker found in the Alaskan wilderness?
    A. The cause of death was listed as hypothermia.
    B. The cause of death was listed as food poisoning.
    C. The cause of death was listed as starvation.
    D. The cause of death was listed as natural causes.

11. How did Westerberg help the authorities locate McCandless's family?
    A. Westerberg gave the authorities McCandless's driver's license, which he had left in his wallet with Westerberg for safe keeping until his return.
    B. Westerberg gave the authorities the home address McCandless had given him to forward his things "in case something happens."
    C. Westerberg told the authorities McCandless's name and that he had lived in the Virginia suburbs of Washington, D.C.
    D. Westerberg gave the authorities McCandless's correct social security number from a W-4 form McCandless completed when he worked for Westerberg.

Part IV

1. How long after Chris's body was discovered did the author interview Walt McCandless?
    A. The interview takes place four weeks later.
    B. The interview takes place two weeks later.
    C. The interview takes place one year later.
    D. The interview takes place seven weeks later.

2. How did Chris's disappearance in 1990 change Walt McCandless?
    A. He became more stern towards his children.
    B. He became more distant from the family.
    C. He became a more tolerant man.
    D. He became obsessively fearful of losing Chris.

3. What event in high school illustrated Chris's determination to follow his own path?
    A. Chris received a failing grade because he refused to write a report in the teacher's prescribed format.
    B. Chris knew exactly how much he could get away with and did as he pleased up to that limit.
    C. Chris paid no attention to the school schedule; he was always in trouble for being tardy.
    D. Chris constantly argued with his teachers over social issues and how they should be dealt with.

4. Identify Loren Johnson.
    A. Loren Johnson was Walt's stepfather, Chris's grandfather, who was a truck driver.
    B. Loren Johnson was Chris's adored grandfather who loved the wilderness.
    C. Loren Johnson was Billie's brother, Chris's uncle, who liked the outdoors.
    D. Loren Johnson was Chris's best friend in high school.

5. What damaged Chris's relationship with Carine?
    A. Carine was better at sports.
    B. Carine was a better French horn player.
    C. Carine was obviously Walt and Billie's favorite child.
    D. Carine told Chris she thought he was crazy for roaming around on his journeys.

6. Who was Buckley?
    A. Buckley helped Chris by giving him a ride.
    B. Buckley was the family dog.
    C. Buckley was Chris's first employer.
    D. Buckley was a high school friend of Chris.

7. Identify Kris Maxie Gillmer.
    A. Gillmer was Chris's closest friend in high school.
    B. Gillmer was Chris's roommate in college.
    C. Gillmer was Chris's half-sister.
    D. Gillmer was Chris's closest friend in college.

8. Which of the following social issues is NOT an issue Chris felt passionate about in high school?
    A. Chris felt passionate about the plight of the homeless.
    B. Chris felt passionate about ecological issues.
    C. Chris felt passionate about apartheid in South Africa.
    D. Chris felt passionate about eliminating hunger.

9. Which of the following activities is NOT one of Chris's entrepreneurial ventures?
    A. At age eight, Chris successfully sold vegetables to the neighbors.
    B. Chris ran his own copy business at age twelve.
    C. Chris got an award for having the most productive paper route at age ten.
    D. In high school, Chris was a top door-to-door salesman for a local contractor.

10. What did Chris do the summer before entering Emory University?
    A. Chris drove across the country.
    B. Chris drove to Alaska.
    C. Chris delivered pizzas.
    D. Chris worked for his parents.

11. After learning his son was lost in the Mojave Desert and nearly died from dehydration, Walt asked Chris to be a little more careful and to keep him better informed of his whereabouts. How did Chris react to his father's concern?
    A. Chris didn't seem to pay any attention to Walt's advice. He smiled and nodded and kept doing exactly what he had been doing.
    B. Chris was angered by this advice. He thought his parents were idiots to worry about him and seemed even less inclined to share his plans.
    C. Chris understood what Walt was trying to say. He grudgingly accepted the advice and tried, for a short while, to keep his parents better informed.
    D. Chris told Walt that his plans were none of his father's business.

12. What did Chris do the summer between his freshman and sophomore years at Emory that helped his parents?
    A. Chris stayed at school where his room and board were covered by his college fund.
    B. Chris made big tips as a waiter in a local restaurant and gave his parents a lot of the money to help out with bills at home.
    C. Chris got a job and worked to support himself.
    D. Chris worked at his parents' business writing computer software.

13. Despite his many skills, what surprising job did Chris take in the summer between his sophomore and junior years at Emory?
    A. Chris worked on a construction crew.
    B. Chris pumped gas.
    C. Chris delivered pizzas.
    D. Chris worked at McDonald's.

14. What did Chris learn about the past that greatly damaged his relationship with his father?
    A. Chris learned that Walt was not really his father. Chris was actually Walt's first wife's illegitimate child. When Walt left Marcia, he got custody of Chris.
    B. Chris learned that his father did not make a clean break with his first wife; he continued the relationship in secret long after he and Billie had Chris.
    C. Chris learned that his father had actually taken "solo journeys," driving and hitchhiking around the country as a young man, without telling anyone of his whereabouts.
    D. Chris learned that his father had abused his first wife. Walt had received counseling and never abused Billie, but Chris was ashamed of his father's weakness, especially since he could tolerate no weakness in Chris.

15. What trip did Chris take the summer between his junior and senior years at Emory?
    A. Chris hitchhiked to California.
    B. Chris drove to Alaska.
    C. Chris drove to South Dakota.
    D. Chris hitchhiked to Colorado.

16. Which statement is NOT true about how Chris's family reacted to his death?
    A. Billie became overprotective of Carine.
    B. Billie gathered pictures of Chris and wept over them.
    C. Walt ate compulsively and gained eight pounds.
    D. Billie lost weight.

Part V

1. As a young man, what adventure did the author fantasize about undertaking?
    A. The author fantasized about conquering remote ascents of various mountains in Alaska and Canada.
    B. The author fantasized about climbing Mt. Everest.
    C. The author fantasized about living alone in the wilderness.
    D. The author fantasized about being the best mountain climber in the world.

2. Why was the author drawn to the Devils Thumb?
    A. The author's father had told him he could successfully climb most mountains-- except the Devils Thumb. Naturally, the author immediately set his sights on that.
    B. Neither his father nor his grandfather had been able to conquer the Devils Thumb. He wanted to show them both up and do something they couldn't do.
    C. The author had made a bet with a friend that he could climb the Devils Thumb. He didn't want to lose the bet.
    D. The north wall of the Devils Thumb had never been conquered, so this mountain was especially interesting to the author.

3. What assets did the author have with him when he departed Boulder to begin his journey to the Devils Thumb?
    A. He had new camping gear, which proved useless.
    B. He had only the clothes on his back.
    C. He had a car and two hundred dollars.
    D. He had a full camper's backpack, warm clothing, and snow shoes.

4. What was the purpose of the pair of aluminum curtain rods the author carried with him on his trek up thirty miles of glaciers to reach the base of the Devils Thumb?
    A. He brought the curtain rods to test the snow's stability.
    B. The curtain rods were spare walking poles.
    C. He intended to use the curtain rods to determine the depth of the snow.
    D. He hoped the curtain rods would span the width of any hidden crevasses he might accidentally come across.

Multiple Choice Questions Part V *Into the Wild* Page 2

5. How did the author transport enough food and gear to the Stikine Ice Cap to last for a three-to-four week stay?
    A. The author used a snowmobile to transport his goods to the base camp.
    B. The author paid a pilot to drop six cartons of supplies at the base of the Devils Thumb.
    C. The author hired a few locals to carry his things to the base of the Devils Thumb. They left him there on his own after the goods were delivered.
    D. The author used a dog sled to travel to the base camp where he stocked in his supplies.

6. Why did the author abandon the climb on the first day?
    A. His gear malfunctioned.
    B. The snow was too heavy.
    C. The wind was too strong to continue climbing safely.
    D. The frost feathers became too thin to continue.

7. What troubled the author the most about the fire in his tent?
    A. He was afraid he would be burned alive.
    B. He wondered what he would do to protect himself from the elements for the remainder of his ordeal.
    C. He wished he had invited someone else to come along who could have helped him in this desperate situation.
    D. He worried that by destroying the tent, he had, once again, lived up to his father's worst expectations.

8. Which item below was NOT a part of the blueprint for success the author's father drew for his children?
    A. He wanted his children to go to the "right" college.
    B. He ultimately wanted his children to attend Harvard Medical School.
    C. He wanted his children to take time for personal reflection and the enjoyment of life.
    D. He wanted his children to excel in all areas of school.

9. Why was the author's father admitted to a psychiatric hospital?
    A. As he aged, his psychiatric condition worsened until he had to be admitted to the psychiatric hospital.
    B. His constant and necessary heavy use of medications caused delusional behavior.
    C. The guilt of his secret past drove him crazy.
    D. Constant worrying sent him over the edge, and he never recovered.

10. Why was the author successful at climbing the Devils Thumb on his last try?
    A. He used sheer willpower to make it. He refused to be unsuccessful on the last try.
    B. He changed his route from the north side of the Devils Thumb to the less dangerous southeast face.
    C. He tried a technique he remembered reading about in *Outdoor* magazine.
    D. He learned from the mistakes he had made on his first attempts.

11. What did the author do once he reached the summit?
    A. He screamed.
    B. He took pictures to prove he was successful.
    C. He planted a flag with his name on it.
    D. He got sick.

12. How did the people of Kito's Kave bar react to the news that the author had successfully climbed the Devils Thumb?
    A. They berated him for doing it, saying it was a foolish thing to do because he could have been killed.
    B. They congratulated him and asked him if he would like to go do it again.
    C. They were very impressed and bought him drinks.
    D. They were not surprised or impressed. Mostly, they did not care.

Multiple Choice Questions Part VI *Into the Wild*

Part VI

1. McCandless planned to hitchhike a thousand miles from Liard to Fairbanks. How far did Gaylord Stuckey drive McCandless?
    A. Stuckey drove McCandless all of the way to Fairbanks.
    B. Stuckey drove McCandless half way.
    C. Stuckey dropped McCandless 20 miles outside of Fairbanks.
    D. Stuckey took McCandless about 300 miles out of Liard.

2. What reason did McCandless give Stuckey for his decision to spend the summer living off the land in the Alaskan bush?
    A. McCandless wanted to prove to himself that he could survive without any help.
    B. McCandless wanted to get as far away from his parents as possible and to have a good excuse not to contact them.
    C. McCandless told Stuckey that he couldn't wait to live in the wilds of Alaska like one of Jack London's heroes.
    D. McCandless told Stuckey that he wanted to live in the woods like Thoreau did.

3. What requests did Stuckey make of McCandless when he dropped him off at the University of Alaska campus?
    A. Stuckey asked McCandless to look him up when he returned from the wild, and to be careful in the bush country, which is full of dangers.
    B. Stuckey asked McCandless to send him a letter when he returned from the wild, and he pleaded with McCandless to call his parents.
    C. Stuckey asked McCandless to get some decent gear before going into the wilderness and to talk with the locals about surviving in Alaska.
    D. Stuckey asked McCandless to take lots of pictures and to keep a journal of his adventures.

4. What item(s) in McCandless's backpack were the heaviest?
    A. McCandless's cookware was the heaviest.
    B. McCandless's clothing was the heaviest.
    C. McCandless's food supplies were the heaviest.
    D. McCandless's paperback books were the heaviest.

5. Why did McCandless decide to make bus 142 his base camp?
    A. The area around the bus was sufficiently isolated from civilization to meet his needs.
    B. McCandless thought the bus would provide the best protection from bears.
    C. The bus was sturdier than a tent.
    D. The bus was located near the river, where he would be more likely to find food.

6. Which of these animals were NOT something McCandless killed for food?
   A. foxes
   B. birds
   C. ducks
   D. moose

7. How did McCandless try (unsuccessfully) to preserve the moose meat?
   A. McCandless tried to freeze the meat.
   B. McCandless tried to smoke the meat.
   C. McCandless tried to can the meat.
   D. McCandless tried to salt the meat.

8. Why could McCandless not leave the bush when he wanted to on July 3rd?
   A. McCandless accidentally trapped himself in the bus.
   B. McCandless was held back by the weather; a bad storm had moved in.
   C. He was too weak from starvation.
   D. He could not safely cross the swollen Teklanika River due to the summer snowmelt from the glaciers.

9. In the author's opinion, what small item did McCandless lack that might have saved his life?
   A. McCandless lacked a proper food storage container.
   B. McCandless lacked a hatchet.
   C. McCandless lacked a good topographic map of the area.
   D. McCandless lacked a compass.

10. Who accompanied the author on his journey to bus 142?
    A. The author traveled with Jan Burres.
    B. The author traveled with Wayne Westerberg, Walt, and Billie.
    C. The author traveled with Roman Dial, Dan Solie, and Andrew Liske.
    D. The author traveled with Walt, Billie, and Carine.

11. How did the author and his companions cross the Teklanika River?
    A. They walked a half-mile to a ranger station where an old wood and rope bridge crossed the river.
    B. They walked a mile to an easy crossing point which was shown on their map.
    C. They crossed the river using an inflatable raft they had brought for that purpose.
    D. They walked a half-mile to an abandoned gauging station where they found a basket on a cable spanning the river.

12. What did the author first see when he entered bus 142?
    A. The author saw the bus swarming with rodents.
    B. The author saw McCandless's diary.
    C. The author saw the mattress where McCandless died.
    D. The author saw McCandless's camera.

13. What was the subject of most of McCandless's journal entries?
    A. McCandless mostly wrote about the weather.
    B. McCandless mostly wrote about philosophical things.
    C. McCandless mostly wrote about food.
    D. McCandless mostly wrote about his family.

14. What was the last book McCandless read?
    A. The last book McCandless read was *The Call of the Wild*.
    B. The last book McCandless read was *Doctor Zhivago*.
    C. The last book McCandless read was *Walden*.
    D. The last book McCandless read was a collection of Tolstoy's stories including "Family Happiness."

15. Why did McCandless begin to eat the seeds rather than the roots of the wild potato?
    A. The roots of the wild potato wither in the summer months.
    B. He thought the seeds would have more nutrients.
    C. He watched the animals eating them and decided to follow their example.
    D. In the summer, the roots of the wild potato become too tough to eat.

16. What food, in the author's opinion, caused McCandless's death?
    A. The author thought that McCandless died from eating wild sweet peas.
    B. The author thought that McCandless died from eating moldy wild potato seeds.
    C. The author thought that McCandless died from spoiled moose meat.
    D. The author thought that McCandless died from eating diseased birds.

17. What significant milestone did McCandless note in his journal even though he was weak and starving?
    A. McCandless noted in his journal that he had climbed the Devils Thumb.
    B. McCandless noted in his journal that he had lived a free and natural life as Thoreau had done.
    C. McCandless noted in his journal that he had survived 100 days in the bush.
    D. McCandless noted in his journal that he had traveled over 10,000 miles on foot.

18. Why did the authorities conclude that McCandless did not vandalize the nearby cabins?
    A. The cabins were on the other side of the Teklanika River; McCandless couldn't have reached them.
    B. The destruction looked more like a wild animal had done it than a human.
    C. The cabins were too far away for McCandless to have reached them.
    D. There was no evidence in McCandless's journal or in his photographs to indicate that he knew about the cabins.

19. McCandless might have been rescued if he had started a forest fire as a distress signal. Why, in his sister Carine's opinion, did McCandless fail to do this?
    A. Carine believed Chris was too weak to go out and start a fire.
    B. Carine believed that her brother probably thought of starting a fire but worried how he could escape the fire himself, being so weak. It may have seemed counter-productive to him.
    C. Carine believed Chris simply didn't think of it; it just never occurred to him to start a fire.
    D. Carine believed that her brother would never burn a forest, even to save his own life.

20. What evidence did McCandless leave behind showing that he was happy before he died?
    A. McCandless's last journal entry said he was happy with the life he had.
    B. The expression on McCandless's face was a happy one.
    C. McCandless left a photograph of himself smiling and holding a note saying he had had a happy life.
    D. McCandless left a note on the bus wall saying farewell and that he was content to die in the wilderness.

21. After visiting the site of their son's death, Billie and Walt went to see bus 142. Which of the following did Billie and Walt NOT leave behind in bus 142?
    A. an emergency kit
    B. a note instructing anyone who found the bus to call his or her parents
    C. an engraved memorial stone
    D. a small brass plaque

ANSWER KEY: MULTIPLE CHOICE QUESTIONS *Into the Wild*

	1	2	3	4	5	6
1	D	B	C	D	A	A
2	A	D	D	C	D	A
3	A	B	A	A	C	B
4	C	C	A	B	D	D
5	A	D	D	B	B	A
6	C	A	D	B	D	A
7	B	D	B	A	D	B
8	C	B	A	B	C	D
9	A	C	A	C	B	C
10	B	A	C	A	B	C
11		D	D	B	B	D
12		C		D	D	C
13		D		C		C
14		D		B		B
15		C		B		D
16		D		A		B
17		C				C
18		B				D
19		B				D
20		C				C
21		C				C
22		D				
23		A				
24		A				
25		A				
26		B				
27		B				

VOCABULARY WORKSHEETS

VOCABULARY PART I *Into the Wild*

Part I: Using Prior Knowledge and Contextual Clues
Below are the sentences in which the vocabulary words appear in the text. Read the sentence. Use any clues you can find in the sentence combined with your prior knowledge, and write what you think the underlined words mean on the lines provided.

1. I spent more than a year retracing the convoluted path that led to his death in the Alaska taiga, chasing down details of his <u>peregrinations</u> with an interest that bordered on obsession.

   _____

2. I do so hope that my experiences will throw some oblique light on the <u>enigma</u> of Chris McCandless.

   _____

3. ...he entertained no illusions that he was trekking into a land of milk and honey; peril, adversity, and Tolstoyan <u>renunciation</u> were precisely what he was seeking.

   _____

4. Some readers admired the boy immensely for his courage and noble ideals; others <u>fulminated</u> that he was a reckless idiot...

   _____

5. ...he was a reckless idiot, a wacko, a <u>narcissist</u> who perished out of arrogance and stupidity...

   _____

6. "People from Outside," reports Gallien in a slow, <u>sonorous</u> drawl, "they'll pick up a copy of *Alaska* magazine, thumb through it, get to thinkin' 'Hey, I'm goin' to get on up there, live off the land, go claim me a piece of the good life.'..."

   _____

7. The trees had been stripped by a recent wind of their white covering of frost, and they seemed to lean toward each other, black and <u>ominous</u>, in the fading light.

   _____

8. A vintage International Harvester from the 1940s, the <u>derelict</u> vehicle is located twenty-five miles west of Healy...rusting incongruously in the fireweed...

   _____

9. ...it harbors more than its share of wolf, bear, caribou, moose, and other game, a local secret that's jealously guarded by those hunters and trappers who are aware of the <u>anomaly</u>.

   _____

10. Thompson, Samel, and Swanson, however, are <u>contumacious</u> Alaskans with a special fondness for driving motor vehicles where motor vehicles aren't really designed to be driven.

    _____

Vocabulary Part I Worksheet *Into the Wild* Page 2

11. Virtually no <u>subcutaneous</u> fat remained on the body, and the muscles had withered significantly...

___

12. At the time of the autopsy, McCandless's remains weighed sixty-seven pounds. Starvation was <u>posited</u> as the most probable cause of death.

___

Part II: Determining the Meaning -- Match the vocabulary words to their dictionary definitions.

____ 1. peregrinations	A.	threatening; foreboding
____ 2. enigma	B.	irregularity; exception
____ 3. renunciation	C.	strongly proposed or assumed; fixed
____ 4. fulminated	D.	travels
____ 5. narcissist	E.	mystery; something difficult to understand
____ 6. sonorous	F.	loud; impressive
____ 7. ominous	G.	stubbornly disobedient
____ 8. derelict	H.	turning away from; self-denial
____ 9. anomaly	I.	abandoned
____ 10. contumacious	J.	self-absorbed person with an inflated self-image
____ 11. subcutaneous	K.	under the skin
____ 12. posited	L.	actively criticized; ranted

ADDITIONAL PART I VOCABULARY *Into the Wild*

taiga – a subarctic forest
muskeg – a bog; an area of decaying vegetation
bug dope – insect repellant
ramparts – rocky wall-like ridges
cordillera – parallel mountain chains or ranges
escarpments – long cliffs created by erosion
glacier – a mass of frozen snow and ice that slowly moves across land
glacial till – material and rock carried and then deposited by a glacier
permafrost – a permanently frozen layer of earth
fording – crossing a shallow body of water by wading
antimony – a metalloid element used in alloys
asceticism – a way of living with only necessities; an existence of self-denial
amalgam – a mixture, a blend, especially of elements

VOCABULARY PART II *Into the Wild*

Part I: Using Prior Knowledge and Contextual Clues

Below are the sentences in which the vocabulary words appear in the text. Read the sentence. Use any clues you can find in the sentence combined with your prior knowledge, and write what you think the underlined words mean on the lines provided.

1. There was something arresting about the youngster's eyes. Dark and <u>emotive</u>, they suggested a trace of exotic blood in his heritage...

   _____

2. His face had a strange <u>elasticity</u>: It would be slack and expressionless one minute, only to twist suddenly into a gaping, oversize grin...

   _____

3. It was almost like a moral thing for him. He was what you'd call extremely <u>ethical</u>. He set pretty high standards for himself.

   _____

4. The living arrangements were loose and <u>convivial</u>. The four or five inhabitants took turns cooking for one another; went drinking together; and chased women together...

   _____

5. He liked the community's stasis, its <u>plebeian</u> virtues and unassuming mien. The place was a back eddy, a pool of jetsam beyond the pull of the main current...

   _____

6. ...he would no longer give or accept gifts. Indeed, Chris had only recently <u>upbraided</u> Walt and Billie for expressing their desire to buy him a new car as a graduation present...

   _____

7. He had spent the previous four years, as he saw it, preparing to fulfill an absurd and <u>onerous</u> duty: to graduate from college.

   _____

8. There was nowhere to move the car, however, as the only route of <u>egress</u> was now a foaming, full-blown river.

   _____

9. My days were more exciting when I was penniless and had to <u>forage</u> around for my next meal.

   _____

10. The journal entries become short and <u>perfunctory</u>. He wrote fewer than a hundred words over the month that followed.

    _____

Vocabulary Part II Worksheet *Into the Wild* Page 2

11. McCandless, nevertheless, took a strong liking to Bullhead. Maybe it was his affinity for the lumpen, who were well represented in the community's trailer parks and campgrounds and laundromats...

12. McCandless conveniently overlooked the fact that London himself had spent just a single winter in the North and that he'd died by his own hand on this California estate at the age of forty, a fatuous drunk...

13. For more than two years the canal inadvertently diverted virtually all of the river's prodigious flow into the Salton sink. Water surged across the once-dry floor of the sink, inundating farms and settlements...

14. One can only speculate about why Franz became so attached to McCandless so quickly, but the affection he felt was genuine, intense, and unalloyed.

15. So on December 26, when I learned what happened, I renounced the Lord. I withdrew my church membership and became an atheist.

16. Nor was McCandless endowed with a surfeit of common sense. Many who knew him have commented, unbidden, that he seemed to have great difficulty seeing the trees, as it were, for the forest.

17. It seems that McCandless was drawn to women but remained largely or entirely celibate, as chaste as a monk.

18. McCandless may have been tempted by the succor offered by women, but it paled beside the prospect of rough congress with nature, with the cosmos itself. And thus was he drawn north, to Alaska.

19. ...Alex has merely run back into the bed of the now dead and dry Colorado River. He discovers another canal about 1/2 mile on the other side of the river bed. He decides to portage to this canal.

20. McCandless spoke frequently to the denizens of the Slabs about his plans for Alaska.

Part II: Determining the Meaning -- Match the vocabulary words to their dictionary definitions.

____ 1. emotive   A. superficial; lacking enthusiasm
____ 2. elasticity   B. common or crude in manner
____ 3. ethical   C. living without ever having sexual intercourse
____ 4. convivial   D. social; enjoying feasting together and good company
____ 5. plebeian   E. unqualified; pure
____ 6. upbraided   F. burdensome
____ 7. onerous   G. the act of coming together
____ 8. egress   H. means of exit; a way out
____ 9. forage   I. ability to be stretched out of shape and readily return to original form
____ 10. perfunctory   J. excess
____ 11. lumpen   K. carry or transport a boat over land
____ 12. fatuous   L. citizens
____ 13. inundating   M. foolish; ridiculous
____ 14. unalloyed   N. flooding; covering
____ 15. atheist   O. one who does not believe in God or any deity
____ 16. surfeit   P. search for food or provisions
____ 17. celibate   Q. of the lower class of society
____ 18. congress   R. criticized; reproached
____ 19. portage   S. conforming to standards of conduct
____ 20. denizens   T. emotionally expressive

ADDITIONAL PART II VOCABULARY *Into the Wild*

mawkish – overly sentimental; romantic
hyperkinetic – overactive
rubber tramps – vagabonds who travel by motorized vehicle
leather tramps – vagabonds who travel by foot
tamarisk – desert shrubs and trees with narrow leaves and flowers
odyssey – a long, wandering quest
hummock – a rounded hill
inimical – hostile
aridity – excessive dryness
concave – rounded inward like the side of a bowl
convection – the transfer of heat resulting in a swirling, circular motion
sere – dried out
oxymoronic – a combination of contradictory elements
bourgeois – relating to the middle class
rheumy – runny, watery
turgid – excessively embellished
anachronistic – chronologically out of place
hegira – a journey to escape unpleasantness
creosote – a desert plant with a sticky resin
desiccated – dried up
phantasmal – delusional
arroyos – a dried creek bed
geothermal – relating to heat from the earth
bajada – Spanish for debris along the slopes of mountains
helter-skelter – haphazard
ocotillo – desert plant with flowers
milo – drought-resistant grain
tundra – a treeless plain with artic or sub artic traits

VOCABULARY Part III *Into the Wild*

Part I: Using Prior Knowledge and Contextual Clues

Below are the sentences in which the vocabulary words appear in the text. Read the sentence. Use any clues you can find in the sentence combined with your prior knowledge, and write what you think the underlined words mean on the lines provided.

1. The article about McCandless in *Outside* generated a large volume of mail, and not a few of the letters heaped <u>opprobrium</u> on McCandless--and on me, as well, the author of the story, for glorifying what some thought was a foolish, pointless death.

   _____

2. "Krakauer is a kook if he doesn't think Chris 'Alexander Supertramp' McCandless was a kook," <u>opined</u> a man from North Pole, Alaska.

   _____

3. The most strident criticism came in the form of a dense, multipage <u>epistle</u> from Ambler...

   _____

4. McCandless is, finally, just a pale 20th-century burlesque of London's protagonist, who freezes because he ignores advice and commits big-time <u>hubris</u>...

   _____

5. In mid-winter a field biologist discovered all of his belongings--two rifles, camping gear, a diary filled with incoherent ranting about truth and beauty and <u>recondite</u> ecological theory....No trace of the young man was ever found.

   _____

6. ...Edward Hoagland observed that Alaska is "not the best site in the world for <u>eremitic</u> experiments or peace-love theatrics."

   _____

7. Rosellini appeared to accept the failure of his hypothesis with <u>equanimity</u>. At the age of forty-nine, he cheerfully announced that he had "recast" his goals...

   _____

8. Waterman was a small person, barely five feet three inches tall, with an elfin face and the <u>sinewy</u>, inexhaustible physique of a gymnast.

   _____

9. He'd [Waterman] take <u>copious</u> notes, creating a complete record of everything he did during the course of each day.

   _____

10. ...McCunn began to worry when nobody arrived to fly him out. "I think I should have used more foresight about arranging my departure," he confessed to his diary, significant portions of which were published <u>posthumously</u> in a five-part story....

    _____

Vocabulary Part III Worksheet *Into the Wild* Page 2

11. In November he finished the last of his rations. He felt weak and dizzy; chills racked his gaunt frame.

   _____

12. Like Rosellini and Waterman, McCandless was a seeker and had an impractical fascination with the harsh side of nature. Like Waterman and McCunn, he displayed a staggering paucity of common sense. But unlike Waterman, McCandless wasn't mentally ill.

   _____

13. ...Ruess was married to a Navajo woman, with whom he'd raised at least one child. The veracity of this and other reports of relatively recent Ruess sightings, needless to say, is extremely suspect.

   _____

Part II: Determining the Meaning -- Match the vocabulary words to their dictionary definitions.

____ 1. opprobrium   A. excessively thin

____ 2. opined   B. plentiful; abundant in number

____ 3. epistle   C. published or done after a person's death

____ 4. hubris   D. truth

____ 5. recondite   E. extreme or exaggerated self-confidence

____ 6. eremitic   F. hermit-like; solitary

____ 7. equanimity   G. calmness; relaxed or balanced state of mind

____ 8. sinewy   H. difficult for ordinary people to understand; obscure

____ 9. copious   I. stringy but strong

____ 10. posthumously   J. formal letter

____ 11. gaunt   K. remarked; commented as in expressing an opinion

____ 12. paucity   L. criticism; judgment

____ 13. veracity   M. scarcity

ADDITIONAL PART III VOCABULARY *Into the Wild*

burlesque -- a ridiculous or extreme interpretation
bight -- a small bay
athapaskan -- a local Alaskan group with their own language
tundra -- a treeless plain with arctic or sub arctic traits
seine -- a large fishing net
defile -- a narrow passage
petroglyphs -- carvings in rock walls
pictographs -- pictures of a past era painted or drawn on rock walls
nom de plume -- French for "pen name"
talus -- a slope formed from rock debris
topography -- the art of representing in detail the elevations, features (both natural and man-made) of an area
stratum -- a layer of rock found between beds of other kinds
curraghs -- small, lightweight, ancient boat
bald -- area without vegetation

VOCABULARY PART IV *Into the Wild*

Part I: Using Prior Knowledge and Contextual Clues

Below are the sentences in which the vocabulary words appear in the text. Read the sentence. Use any clues you can find in the sentence combined with your prior knowledge, and write what you think the underlined words mean on the lines provided.

1. Money was tight. In addition to the financial strain of exchanging a steady paycheck for the <u>vagaries</u> of self-employment, Walt's separation from his first wife left him with two families to support.

   _____

2. ...he [Chris] can be heard belting out "Summers by the sea/Sailboats in Capri" with impressive <u>panache</u>, crooning like a professional lounge singer.

   _____

3. ...he [Chris] became obsessed with racial oppression in South Africa. He spoke seriously to his friends about smuggling weapons into that country and joining the struggle to end <u>apartheid</u>.

   _____

4. ...he [Chris] had a darker side as well, characterized by <u>monomania</u>, impatience, and unwavering self-absorption...

   _____

5. ...Chris apparently judged artists and close friends by their work, not their life, yet he was temperamentally incapable of extending such <u>lenity</u> to his father.

   _____

6. ...Chris would fixate on his father's own less than sterling behavior many years earlier and silently denounce him as a <u>sanctimonious</u> hypocrite.

   _____

7. Chris kept careful score. And over time he worked himself into a <u>choler</u> of self-righteous indignation that was impossible to keep bottled up.

   _____

8. ...he [Chris] authored scores of commentaries....The opinions he expressed in print, argued with <u>idiosyncratic</u> logic, were all over the map.

   _____

9. He <u>lampooned</u> Jimmy Carter and Joe Biden, called for the resignation of Attorney General Edwin Meese...

   _____

10. He lampooned Jimmy Carter and Joe Biden, called for the resignation of Attorney General Edwin Meese, <u>lambasted</u> Bible-thumpers of the Christian right...

    _____

Vocabulary Part IV Worksheet *Into the Wild* Page 2

11. He lampooned Jimmy Carter and Joe Biden, called for the resignation of Attorney General Edwin Meese, lambasted Bible-thumpers of the Christian right, and urged vigilance against the soviet threat, <u>castigated</u> the Japanese for hunting whales, and defended Jessee Jackson as a viable presidential candidate.

    _____

12. As soon as classes ended in the spring of 1989, Chris took his Datsun on another prolonged <u>extemporaneous</u> road trip.

    _____

13. ...but he had been smitten by the vastness of the land, by the ghostly hue of the glaciers, by the <u>pellucid</u> subarctic sky.

    _____

14. ...weeping as only a mother who has outlived a child can weep....Such bereavement, witnessed at close range, makes even the most eloquent <u>apologia</u> for high-risk activities ring fatuous and hollow.

    _____

Part II: Determining the Meaning -- Match the vocabulary words to their dictionary definitions.

____ 1. vagaries   A. eccentric; peculiar
____ 2. panache   B. style; flamboyance
____ 3. apartheid   C. defense of one's own actions
____ 4. monomania   D. translucently clear
____ 5. lenity   E. reproached; rebuked
____ 6. sanctimonious   F. anger
____ 7. choler   G. excessive fixation on a single idea
____ 8. idiosyncratic   H. berated; chewed-out
____ 9. lampooned   I. leniency; acceptance; tolerance
____ 10. lambasted   J. unplanned; impromptu
____ 11. castigated   K. satirized; ridiculed
____ 12. extemporaneous   L. falsely pious or devout
____ 13. pellucid   M. uncertainties
____ 14. apologia   N. a policy of racial segregation in South Africa

VOCABULARY PART V *Into the Wild*

Part I: Using Prior Knowledge and Contextual Clues

Below are the sentences in which the vocabulary words appear in the text. Read the sentence. Use any clues you can find in the sentence combined with your prior knowledge, and write what you think the underlined words mean on the lines provided.

1. What distinguished that summit above the earthly line, is that it is <u>unhandselled</u>, awful, grand. It can never become familiar; you are lost the moment you set foot there.

   _____

2. The Devils Thumb <u>demarcates</u> the Alaska-British Columbia border east of Petersburg, a fishing village accessible only by boat or plane.

   _____

3. So I drove as far as Gig Harbor, Washington, abandoned the car, and <u>inveigled</u> a ride on a northbound salmon seiner.

   _____

4. Here the glacier spills abruptly over the edge of a high plateau, dropping seaward through a gap between two mountains in a <u>phantasmagoria</u> of shattered ice.

   _____

5. My efforts were lent a sense of urgency by the noises emanating from beneath my feet. A <u>madrigal</u> of creaks and sharp reports...

   _____

6. The rock, exhibiting a <u>dearth</u> of holds and coated with six inches of crumbly rime, did not look promising...

   _____

7. A kind and generous man, Lewis Krakauer loved his five children deeply, in the <u>autocratic</u> way of fathers, but his worldview was colored by a relentlessly competitive nature.

   _____

8. He was ambitious in the extreme, and like Walt McCandless, his aspirations extended to his <u>progeny</u>.

   _____

9. From elementary school through high school, my siblings and I were <u>hectored</u> to excel in every class, to win medals in science fairs, to be chosen princess of the prom, to win election to student government.

   _____

Vocabulary Part V Worksheet *Into the Wild* Page 2

10. I saw that I had been selfish and unbending and a giant pain in the ass. He'd built a bridge of privilege for me, a hand-paved trestle to the good life, and I repaid him by chopping it down and crapping on the wreckage. But this <u>epiphany</u> occurred only after the intervention of time and misfortune...

___

11. Crippled muscles withered further, synapses wouldn't fire, wasted legs refused to <u>ambulate</u>.

___

12. By the late afternoon the squall had <u>metastasized</u> into another major storm.

___

13. ...it was no longer possible to ignore the fact that the Thumb had made hash of my plans. I was forced to acknowledge that <u>volition</u> alone, however powerful, was not going to get me up the north wall.

___

14. At the time, I'd considered this route unworthy of my attentions. Now, on the rebound from my <u>calamitous</u> entanglement with the *norwand*, I was prepared to lower my sights.

___

Part II: Determining the Meaning -- Match the vocabulary words to their dictionary definitions.

____ 1.	unhandselled	A.	walk; move from place to place
____ 2.	demarcates	B.	dominating; bossy; dictatorial
____ 3.	inveigled	C.	offspring; children
____ 4.	phantasmagoria	D.	distinguishes; sets apart
____ 5.	madrigal	E.	spread; grown
____ 6.	dearth	F.	determination; will
____ 7.	autocratic	G.	fantastic images seen as if in a dream
____ 8.	progeny	H.	lack of; shortage
____ 9.	hectored	I.	wangled; acquired through ingenuity
____ 10.	epiphany	J.	song with several unaccompanied voices singing in harmony
____ 11.	ambulate	K.	sudden realization; illuminating discovery or understanding
____ 12.	metastasized	L.	disasterous
____ 13.	volition	M.	intimidated; bullied
____ 14.	calamitous	N.	unforgiving

ADDITIONAL PART V VOCABULARY *Into The Wild*

norwand – the north wall of a mountain
desideratum – desired, felt to be essential
carapace – a protective shell
cirque – at the base of a mountain, a deep area with walls
crampons – metal spike-like prongs strapped to mountain climbing boots to grip ice
bergschrund – a split in the ice; a crevasse
rime – granular ice formed by the cooling of fog
gunwale – the upper edge of a ship's side
seracs – peaks along the ridge of a glacier
bivouac (bivvy) – a temporary camp with little or no shelter
verglas – heavy glacial ice
spindrift – fine snow carried by strong wind

VOCABULARY PART VI *Into the Wild*

Part I: Using Prior Knowledge and Contextual Clues

Below are the sentences in which the vocabulary words appear in the text. Read the sentence. Use any clues you can find in the sentence combined with your prior knowledge, and write what you think the underlined words mean on the lines provided.

1. ...the river's volume was quite low when McCandless crossed....He never suspected that in so doing, he was crossing his <u>Rubicon</u>. ...there was nothing to suggest that two months hence, as the glaciers and snowfields at the Teklanika's headwater thawed in the summer heat, its discharge would multiply nine or ten times in volume...

   _____

2. Moreover, as the ground thawed, his route turned into a gauntlet of boggy muskeg and impenetrable alder, and McCandless belated came to appreciate one of the fundamental (if counterintuitive) <u>axioms</u> of the North: winter, not summer, is the preferred season for traveling overland through the bush.

   _____

3. Overjoyed, the proud hunter took a photograph of himself kneeling over his trophy, rifle thrust triumphantly overhead, his features distorted in a <u>rictus</u> of ecstasy and amazement...

   _____

4. Attempting to swim the numbingly cold torrent or even to paddle some sort of improvised raft across seemed too risky to consider...but by dog-paddling and hopping along the bottom...he could conceivably have made it across before being carried into the gorge or succumbing to <u>hypothermia</u>.

   _____

5. What the angry letter writers didn't know, however, was that the <u>ungulate</u> McCandless shot was exactly what he'd said it was. Contrary to what I reported in *Outside*, the animal was a moose...

   _____

6. A few inches away sits a skull the size of a watermelon, thick ivory fangs jutting from its bleached <u>maxillae</u>. It is a bear skull...

   _____

7. I feel uncomfortable, as if I were intruding, a <u>voyeur</u> who has slipped into McCandless's bedroom while he is momentarily away.

   _____

8. He had been woefully unprepared to lead an Arctic expedition, and upon returning to England, he was known as the Man Who Ate His Shoes--yet the <u>sobriquet</u> was uttered more often with awe than with ridicule.

   _____

Vocabulary Part VI Worksheet *Into the Wild* Page 2

9. In the last three weeks of July, he killed thirty-five squirrels, four spruce grouse, five jays and woodpeckers, and two frogs....But despite this apparent <u>munificence</u>, the meat he'd been killing was very lean, and he was consuming fewer calories than he was burning.

_____

10. ...Hedysarum mackenzii is poisonous, and nearly killed an old Indian woman...Fortunately, it proved <u>emetic</u>; and her stomach having rejected all that she had swallowed, she was restored to health, though her recovery was for some time doubtful.

_____

11. The effects of swainsonine poisoning are chronic--the alkaloid rarely kills outright. The toxin does the deed <u>insidiously</u>, indirectly, by inhibiting an enzyme essential to glycoprotein metabolism....The body is prevented from turning what it eats into a source of usable energy.

_____

12. ...there's no way to flush the toxin from your system. When a starving mammal ingests an alkaloid--even one as benign as caffeine--it's going to get hit much harder by it than it normally would because they lack the glucose reserves necessary to <u>excrete</u> the stuff. The alkaloid is simply going to accumulate in the system.

_____

Part II: Determining the Meaning -- Match the vocabulary words to their dictionary definitions.

____ 1. Rubicon   A. abnormally low body temperature
____ 2. axioms   B. eliminate from blood, organs, tissues
____ 3. rictus   C. animal with hooves
____ 4. hypothermia   D. upper jaw of an animal
____ 5. ungulate   E. nickname
____ 6. maxillae   F. abundance; plenty
____ 7. voyeur   G. established truths, rules, or principles
____ 8. sobriquet   H. dangerously subtle; developing very slowly until it is too late
____ 9. munificence   I. something that causes vomiting
____ 10. emetic   J. line or boundary that is irrevocable once it is crossed
____ 11. insidiously   K. someone who spies on another's personal life
____ 12. excrete   L. open-mouthed grin

ADDITIONAL VOCABULARY PART VI *Into the Wild*

ethnobotany – the study of plant knowledge acquired over time by a culture
geophysical – the study of the physical properties of the Earth
sulfurous – usually refers to the stink of the chemical sulfur
coppice – a grove
hydrologists – the study of water above and below the Earth's surface
massif – a major mountain range
miasma – fog
fecund – fruitful
feral – wild, undomesticated
glucose – sugar

VOCABULARY ANSWER KEY - *Into the Wild*

	1	2	3	4	5	6	
1	D	T	L	M	N	J	
2	E	I	K	B	D	G	
3	H	S	J	N	I	L	
4	L	D	E	G	G	A	
5	J	B	H	I	J	C	
6	F	R	F	L	H	D	
7	A	F	G	F	B	K	
8	I	H	I	A	C	E	
9	B	P	B	K	M	F	
10	G	A	C	H	K	I	
11	K	Q	A	E	A	H	
12	C	M	M	J	E	B	
13		N	D	D	F		
14		E		C	L		
15		O					
16		J					
17		C					
18		G					
19		K					
20		L					

DAILY LESSONS

LESSON ONE

<u>Objectives</u>
1. To introduce the *Into the Wild* unit
2. To distribute books and other materials
3. To preview the study questions and vocabulary for Part I

<u>Preparation</u>
Prior to this lesson, prepare your bulletin board with a large map of the United States, including Alaska, with an appropriate heading. For example, the heading might be *Into the Wild*: McCandless's Route to Alaska. You will need push-pins. As the unit progresses, the push-pins will be used to map McCandless's meandering route to Alaska. Maps, which can be used as a guide for McCandless's journey, are provided in the book.

<u>Activity #1</u>
Explain to students that *Into the Wild* is a nonfiction account of Chris McCandless's solo journey across the country. As he traveled, he slowly divested himself of most of his belongings. Ultimately, he entered the Alaskan bush with only the items he could carry in his backpack.

Ask students to make a list of the essential items they would pack for a solo trek into the Alaskan wilderness, using their school backpacks as a guide for how much they could take. The list must include food (or a means to acquire food), clothing, weapons, personal items, reference material, and entertainment. All of the items selected must fit into the backpack and be light enough to be carried. This activity can be completed in small groups. Each group will present its agreed-upon list to the class for critique.

TRANSITION: Explain to the class that the book was written after the young man's decomposing body was found in the Alaskan wilderness. The author traces McCandless's journey, and the reasons for this journey, through first person accounts, McCandless's journal, and by reflecting on the author's own life experiences.

<u>Activity #2</u>
Distribute the materials students will use in this unit. Explain in detail how students are to use these materials.

<u>Activity #3</u>
Preview the study questions and have students do the vocabulary work for Part I of *Into the Wild*. If students do not finish this assignment during this class period, they should complete it prior to the next class meeting.

NOTE: *Students will preview the study questions and vocabulary prior to each reading selection. Vary the methods of doing this throughout the unit based on your class, your preferences, and the time available. Some variations include using small groups, student pairs, individual work, or whole class participation.*

LESSON TWO

Objectives
1. To read the Author's Note
2. To predict content
3. To read Part I

Activity #1
Have students read the Author's Note in whatever way you choose: orally, silently, in small groups, etc.

Activity #2
In the Author's Note, Krakauer lists three reasons for writing this book:

1. The author was "haunted by the particulars of the boy's starvation and by vague, unsettling parallels between events in his life and those in my own."

2. The author reflected on "the allure high-risk activities hold for young men of a certain mind..."

3. The author also reflected on the "highly charged bond that exists between fathers and sons."

Explain to students that the author's reasons for writing the book provide the reader with a preview of the book's content. In a group discussion, ask students to predict the possible content of the coming chapters. There are no wrong answers to this activity. The goal is to engage students' interest in reading further.

Activity #3
Read Part I orally, silently, or in small groups. If students do not complete reading Part I in class, they should do so prior to your next class meeting.

LESSON THREE

Objectives
1. To review the main ideas and events in Part I
2. To do the pre-reading work for Part II
3. To read Part II

Activity #1
Using the study questions for Part I as a guide, discuss the main events and ideas from Part I.

After each reading assignment in this unit, class time is devoted to discussing the main events and ideas from each section. Use a variety of teaching techniques to accomplish this task so students have a variety of approaches to covering the materials. Rather than specify a particular technique for each review session, this unit allows you the freedom to choose the method you wish to use for each review session.

Here are some ideas as to different approaches to take:

Quiz: Use the multiple choice study questions as a quiz. As you check the quizzes in class, have students use the short answer study guides to take more extensive notes about each question. Students can swap papers to correct the multiple choice quizzes, or you can collect them for teacher grading.

Small Groups: Assign a few of the study questions to small groups of 3 students. Give students ample time to discuss the questions in their groups and to formulate answers. Come together as a whole class to discuss the answers to all of the questions.

Independent Work: Have each student answer all of the questions independently on paper, then come together as a whole group to discuss all of the questions and answers.

Whole Class: Discuss each study question as a whole class, having students take notes as the discussion progresses.

Interactive Whiteboard: As you discuss the questions, take notes on your interactive whiteboard and then save the file with the answers for students to access for study purposes. Have students take turns being the note scribe.

From A Hat: Make a copy of the study questions and cut each question apart onto its own strip of paper. Fold each paper to hide the question and put the papers in a hat. Pass the hat for each student to pull out a question to answer. You can do a musical chairs version of this activity by playing music as the hat is being passed, and the student who has the hat when the music stops has to choose a question to answer.

These are just a few ideas to get you started. You can use whatever creative approaches you want as long as the questions are reviewed and discussed.

Activity #2
Give students an appropriate amount of time to preview the study questions and to do the vocabulary work for Part II. You may have students work independently or in small groups to complete these activities.

When students have had ample time to complete the pre-reading work, discuss the answers to the vocabulary worksheets so all students have the correct answers for study purposes.

Activity #3

Have students read Part II of *Into the Wild*. This activity may be done silently, orally, independently, or in small groups--however you choose.

If students do not finish reading Part II in the remaining class time, they should do so independently prior to the next class meeting.

LESSON FOUR

Objectives
1. To review the main ideas and events in Part II
2. To map McCandless's route for Parts I and II
3. To explore the relationships between the characters
4. To preview the study questions and vocabulary for Part III

Activity #1
Review the main events and ideas in Part II by discussing the study questions for this section.

Activity #2
As a group, using push pins, trace McCandless's route from Parts I and II on the bulletin board beginning at Emory University in Atlanta. Include the following locations:

Atlanta, GA
Carthage, SD
Orick Beach, CA
Bullhead City, AZ
Niland, CA
Salton City, CA
Carthage, SD
Fairbanks, AK

Activity #3
Distribute the First Person Encounters Chart. Students are to complete the chart for Parts I and II by briefly describing each person's relationship/encounter with McCandless.

This can be done as a whole class using your whiteboard, in small groups, or individually, whichever you choose.

If it is done individually or in small groups, give students ample time to complete the assignment and then discuss the answers.

Activity #4
Preview the study questions and do the vocabulary worksheet for Part II orally as a whole class activity. Make sure students have the correct answers to the vocabulary worksheet for Part II.

NAME _____ DATE _____

FIRST PERSON ENCOUNTERS WITH MCCANDLESS
Into the Wild

NAME	LOCATION OF FIRST ENCOUNTER	RELATIONSHIP/ENCOUNTER
Jim Gallien	Fairbanks, AK	
Wayne Westerberg	Carthage, SD	
Crazy Ernie	Northern California	
Jan Burres & Bob	Orick Beach, CA	
Lori Zarza	Bullhead City, AZ	
Charlie	Bullhead City, AZ	
Tracy	Niland, CA	
Ronald Franz	Salton City, CA	
Gail Borah	Carthage, SD	
Mary Westerberg	Carthage, SD	

FIRST PERSON ENCOUNTERS WITH MCCANDLESS
Into the Wild
ANSWER KEY

NAME	LOCATION OF FIRST ENCOUNTER	RELATIONSHIP/ENCOUNTER
Jim Gallien	Fairbanks, AK	Gallien picked up hitchhiking McCandless and drove him to Anchorage, AK. He tried to talk McCandless out of his plans to live off the land in the Alaskan wild.
Wayne Westerberg	Carthage, SD	Westerberg became a close friend of McCandless after giving him a ride and a job at a grain elevator.
Crazy Ernie	Northern California	Crazy Ernie offered McCandless a job on a ranch in northern CA. McCandless left after eleven days because Ernie never paid him for his work.
Jan Burres & Bob	Orick Beach, CA	Burres and Bob were "rubber tramps" who traveled around the West selling knick-knacks. They gave McCandless a ride. He stayed with them at Orick Beach for a week.
Lori Zarza	Bullhead City, AZ	Lori was the assistant manager of the McDonald's restaurant where McCandless worked.
Charlie	Bullhead City, AZ	Charlie was a co-worker at McDonald's. He let McCandless stay in an old trailer.
Tracy	Niland, CA	Tracy was a seventeen-year-old girl who had a crush on McCandless. She worked at the McDonald's.
Ronald Franz	Salton City, CA	Franz was an eighty-one-year-old man who developed a strong bond with McCandless and wanted to adopt him.
Gail Borah	Carthage, SD	Gail was Westerberg's girlfriend.
Mary Westerberg	Carthage, SD	Mary Westerberg was Wayne Westerberg's mother.

LESSON FIVE

Objectives
1. To review the vocabulary for Part III
2. To practice writing to inform
3. To explore and compare characters in the story
4. To practice logical and critical thinking skills
5. To read Part III

Activity #1
Review the vocabulary worksheets for Part III. Students should have completed the worksheets already; this is just to make sure everyone has the correct answers to study from.

Activity #2
Distribute Writing Assignment #1. Discuss the directions in detail and give students the remainder of this class period to complete the assignment.

If students do not complete the assignment in class, they should do so prior to the next class meeting.

Activity #3
When students finish Writing Assignment #1, they should begin reading Part III. If they do not finish this assignment in class, they should do so prior to your next class meeting.

WRITING ASSIGNMENT #1 *Into the Wild*

PROMPT
The author received a "large volume of mail" from critics of McCandless for being "foolish" and the author for "glorifying" McCandless's death. Krakauer wrote:

The prevailing Alaska wisdom held that McCandless was simply one more dreamy, half-cocked greenhorn who went into the country expecting to find answers to all of his problems and instead found only mosquitoes and a lonely death.

In an effort to defend McCandless, Krakauer described several characters that, like McCandless, perished in the Alaskan wilderness. Write a letter from one of the following characters to Krakauer explaining why the character attempted to survive alone in the Alaskan wild. The letter should be based on information in the book.

Choose one: Gene Rosellini, John Mallon Waterman, Carl McCunn, Everett Ruess

PREWRITING

After selecting a character, reread the section in the book describing his adventure. Make notes of any passages in which the author explains or justifies the character's behavior. In addition, make notes of any passages where the author compares the characters to McCandless.

DRAFTING
Write an introductory paragraph introducing the character you chose to Krakauer. Provide any factual information found in the text. If possible, include name, age, occupation, date of adventure, etc. State the character's reasons for writing to Krakauer.

Write a paragraph for each reason presented in the text for the character's decision to live in the Alaskan wild.

Write a concluding paragraph and sign the letter.

PROMPT
After you finish your letter and are satisfied with it, hand it to a reliable classmate to read. Your classmate should tell you what is good about your letter and things that could be improved.

Considering your classmate's comments, decide what revisions you need to do, and do them.

PROOFREADING
Proofread your revised copy and make any necessary corrections to create a perfect, final copy for grading.

WRITING EVALUATION FORM *Into the Wild*

Student Name _____ Date _____

Writing Assignment # _____

	Excellent	Very Good	Good	Fair	Poor
Content	5	4	3	2	1
Grammar	5	4	3	2	1
Spelling	5	4	3	2	1
Legibility	5	4	3	2	1
Punctuation	5	4	3	2	1
Form	5	4	3	2	1
	5	4	3	2	1
	5	4	3	2	1
	5	4	3	2	1

Comments:

Teacher _____ Grade _____

LESSON SIX

<u>Objectives</u>
1. To review the main events and ideas from Part III
2. To conclude Writing Assignment #1 with oral presentations and discussions of the letters written
3. To preview the study questions and vocabulary for Part IV
4. To introduce the unit Nonfiction Reading Project
5. To explore ways and reasons why people do dangerous things
6. To give students experience researching a predetermined topic
7. To give students practice reading nonfiction
8. To engage students' critical thinking skills
9. To read Part IV

<u>Activity #1</u>
Distribute the Multiple Choice Questions for Part III as a quiz. Give students ample time to answer the questions.

Have students swap papers for grading purposes.

Discuss the answers orally as a class. Ask students to identify the correct answer for any questions where the answer is incorrect on the papers they are evaluating.

When all questions have been discussed, students should return the papers to their owners and then papers should be collected for your review and/or recording of the grades.

<u>Activity #2</u>
Ask for a few volunteers who are willing to read their letters from Writing Assignment #1. Allow ample time for one letter from each different character possibility in the assignment to be read.

Take a few minutes to discuss things the characters had in common and ways in which they were different.

Collect the writing assignments for grading.

<u>Activity #3</u>
Preview the study questions and vocabulary for Part IV orally as a whole class activity.

<u>Activity #4</u>
Distribute the Research Project. Discuss the directions in detail. Give students the remainder of this class period to work on this assignment.

Make research resources available to students, either through Internet access in your classroom, or by taking them to your school's media center or library where they can find the required information.

If time is short after completing the other activities scheduled for this day, you may want to simply introduce and discuss the Research Project rather than actually beginning work on it. There will be time in the next class period for working on the project.

Activity #5
Make the assignment that students should read Part IV. This does not have to be done prior to the next class period, but it should be done prior to Lesson 8.

NONFICTION RESEARCH PROJECT *Into the Wild*

PROMPT
We know from the first page of *Into the Wild* that McCandless died alone in the Alaskan wilderness. He chose to embark on this adventure regardless of the danger or the effects his actions might have had on others.

ASSIGNMENT
Locate an article about a young person, like McCandless, who embarked on a dangerous activity or adventure. Do not limit yourself to articles about adventures in the wilderness. Consider any activity that was potentially harmful to the participant.

Read the article and complete the Journalism Check List. Be prepared to present a five-minute summary of your article to the class, including your opinion of the young person's actions.

JOURNALISM CHECK LIST *Into the Wild*

A well-written news article will answer each of the following questions. Complete this Journalism Check List with facts from the article you chose for the nonfiction research project.

Factual Details in the Article

Who? Who is the article about?

What? What did this person do?

When? When did this event take place?

Where? Where did this event take place?

Why? Why did this person do it?

How? How did this person do it?

Interpretation

What impact did this young person's actions have on his or her family or friends?

In your opinion, to what extent were his or her actions reckless?

Personal Response

What did you learn from this article that you might be able to apply to your life?

LESSON SEVEN

Objectives
1. To give students time to work on the Nonfiction Research Project
2. To complete reading Part IV

Activity #1
Give students access to the materials they need to complete the Nonfiction Research Project; take them to the library or media center or give them Internet access in your classroom.

Students should use this class time to work on and complete the project.

Activity #2
If students complete the research project prior to the end of the class period, they should continue reading Part IV of *Into the Wild*. Remind students that this reading assignment should be completed prior to the next class meeting.

LESSON EIGHT

Objectives
1. To review the main events and ideas in Part IV
2. To conclude the Non-Fiction Research Project with students' oral presentations

Activity #1
Review the main events and ideas in Part IV of *Into the Wild* by discussing the study questions for this section.

Activity #2
Use the remainder of this class time for students to do the oral presentation part of their research projects. Students have a maximum of five minutes (or whatever limit you set) to orally give a summary of the article and to express their opinions about the article. Invite discussion as time permits or as situations warrant it.

An evaluation form is included for your convenience. You can make copies and fill out one evaluation form for each student.

ORAL PRESENTATION EVALUATION
Into the Wild

Student Name _____ Date _____

SKILL	Excellent	Good	Average	Fair	Poor
Content Coverage	5	4	3	2	1
Opinion Coverage	5	4	3	2	1
Audibility	5	4	3	2	1
Diction	5	4	3	2	1
Body Language	5	4	3	2	1
Eye Contact	5	4	3	2	1
Engaging Audience	5	4	3	2	1
	5	4	3	2	1
	5	4	3	2	1
	5	4	3	2	1

Comments:

Teacher _____ Grade _____

LESSON NINE

Objectives
1. To preview the study questions and vocabulary for Part V
2. To evaluate students' oral reading
3. To read Part V

Activity #1
Preview the study questions and do the vocabulary work for Part V of *Into the Wild*. You can do this orally as a whole class activity, in small groups, as individual work, or in any creative way you wish. However it is done, students should read through the questions and complete the vocabulary worksheet for Part V.

Activity #2
Read Part V of *Into the Wild* orally in class, having students take turns reading. If you have not yet completed an oral reading evaluation for your students, this is a great time to do so. A form for this purpose is included in this unit. Simply make copies and fill one out for each student as he or she reads orally. Record the grades if you choose, or simply give the evaluation to the students as feedback for learning purposes.

ORAL READING EVALUATION

Name _____ Date _____

Book _____

	Excellent	**Good**	**Average**	**Fair**	**Poor**
Fluency					
Clarity					
Audibility					
Pronunciation					
Expression					

Grade _____

Comments:

LESSON TEN

Objectives
1. To review the main events and ideas from Part V
2. To practice persuasive writing skills
3. To study the character of Chris McCandless in more depth
4. To think critically about McCandless's actions and motives
5. To preview the study questions and vocabulary for Part VI

Activity #1
Review the main events and ideas of Part V by discussing the study questions for Part V.

Activity #2
Distribute Writing Assignment #2. Discuss the directions in detail and give students ample time to complete the assignment. Remember to tell students when the assignment will be due (at the end of class, in the next class meeting, etc.).

Activity #3
If students complete the writing assignment prior to the end of class, they should preview the study questions and do the vocabulary worksheet for Part VI. This assignment should be completed prior to the next class meeting.

WRITING ASSIGNMENT #2 *Into the Wild*

PROMPT
In Chapter fifteen, the author writes:

As a young man, I was unlike McCandless in many important regards; most notably, I possessed neither his intellect nor his lofty ideals. But I believe we were similarly affected by the skewed relationships we had with our fathers. And I suspect we had a similar intensity, a similar heedlessness, a similar agitation of the soul.

The fact that I survived my Alaska adventure and McCandless did not survive his was largely a matter of chance; had I not returned from the Stikine Ice Cap in 1977, people would have been quick to say of me--as they now say of him--that I had a death wish. Eighteen years after the event, I now recognize that I suffered from hubris, perhaps, and an appalling innocence, certainly; but I wasn't suicidal.

Do you agree with the author's opinion that McCandless was not suicidal? Your assignment is to write an essay defending your position. Be careful to use facts about McCandless's life and death to support your conclusions.

PREWRITING
First, decide if you agree or disagree with the author. Then, make a list of reasons, facts, and events from the text that support your ideas.

DRAFTING
Write an introductory paragraph clearly stating your position. Then, write a paragraph for each supporting detail you found in the text. Be certain to write a topic sentence for each of these paragraphs. Finally, write a concluding paragraph summarizing your ideas. If your arguments are well-supported by facts, your reader should be agreeing with you at this point!

PROOFREADING
Carefully proofread your rough draft for grammar, spelling, organization, and the clarity of your ideas. If possible, ask another student to read your work. He or she should tell you if your arguments were persuasive or if there were any flaws in your logic. Make a final copy of your work including any necessary corrections.

LESSON ELEVEN

Objectives
1. To complete mapping McCandless s route
2. To review the vocabulary work for Part VI
3. To read Part VI

Activity #1
On the bulletin board, complete mapping McCandless's route. Include the following locations: Seattle, WA; Dawson Creek, Canada; Liard River Hotsprings, Canada; and the Stampede Trail.

Discuss the route and terrain and ask students how they would have felt making this trek.

Activity #2
Students should have completed the pre-reading work for Part VI prior to this class period. Take a few minutes to check their vocabulary work to make sure they have the correct answers to study. Do this in whatever way you feel best suits your class and time allotment.

Activity #3
Use this class period to read Part VI. If you have not yet completed the oral reading evaluations, this is a good opportunity to do so. If you have completed the evaluations, students could read orally to each other in small groups (2 or 3 students), or students could practice their silent reading skills.

Students should finish reading Part VI prior to the next class meeting.

LESSON TWELVE

Objectives
1. To review the main events and ideas in Part VI
2. To introduce the Interview Character Role-Playing activity
3. To explore the characters of Carine, Walt, and Billie in more depth
4. To study point of view
5. To exercise critical thinking skills

Activity #1
Review the main events and ideas in Part VI by discussing the study questions for this section. Use whatever approach seems best to you for the time you have to devote to this activity.

Activity #2
Divide your class into three groups: Group Carine, Group Walt, and Group Billie. Explain to the class that this is an Interview Character Role-Playing Activity. Each group will be responsible to prepare to answer interview questions from the point of view of the assigned character. In addition, each group will prepare interview questions for one of the other groups.

Distribute the Character Role-Playing Activity assignment and discuss the directions in detail. Give students the remainder of this class time to work on this assignment.

Students should be prepared to actually do the interviews in the next class meeting.

INTERVIEW CHARACTER ROLE-PLAYING ACTIVITY ASSIGNMENT *Into the Wild*

THE ASSIGNMENT
Your class has been divided into three groups: Group Carine, Group Walt, and Group Billie.

In class today, you will choose one group member to role-play the character for whom your group is named. That person will be interviewed by a member of another group in class in the next class meeting.

Your assignment today is to prepare your character for the interview by creating possible interview questions that might be asked to your character--and answering them.

In addition, each group will appoint one member to be an investigative reporter to interview the character from another group in our next class meeting. In preparation for that, the whole group should brainstorm good questions to ask.

Group Carine
1. Appoint one person to role-play Carine for the interview in the next class meeting.
2. Brainstorm a list of questions a good investigative reporter might ask Carine about the death of her brother.
3. Prepare answers to those questions based on information from the text.
4. Appoint one person to role-play an investigative reporter whose job it will be to interview Billie in the next class period.
5. Brainstorm a list of questions a good investigative reporter might ask Billie. These are the questions your reporter will use to interview Billie in the next class period.

Group Billie
1. Appoint one person to role-play Billie for the interview in the next class meeting.
2. Brainstorm a list of questions a good investigative reporter might ask Billie about the death of her son.
3. Prepare answers to those questions based on information from the text.
4. Appoint one person to role-play an investigative reporter whose job it will be to interview Walt in the next class period.
5. Brainstorm a list of questions a good investigative reporter might ask Walt. These are the questions your reporter will use to interview Walt in the next class period.

Group Walt
1. Appoint one person to role-play Walt for the interview in the next class meeting.
2. Brainstorm a list of questions a good investigative reporter might ask Walt about the death of his son.
3. Prepare answers to those questions based on information from the text.
4. Appoint one person to role-play an investigative reporter whose job it will be to interview Carine in the next class period.
5. Brainstorm a list of questions a good investigative reporter might ask Carine. These are the questions your reporter will use to interview Carine in the next class period.

INTERVIEW CHARACTER ROLE-PLAYING WORKSHEET: CARINE *Into the Wild*

Group Carine

List Group Members:

Who will role-play Carine? _____

Who will role-play the investigative reporter for Billie? _____

Question 1:

Answer to Question 1:

Question 2:

Answer to Question 2:

Question 3:

Answer to Question 3:

Question 4:

Answer to Question 4:

Group Carine Worksheet Page 2
Question 5:

Answer to Question 5:

Question 6:

Answer to Question 6:

Question 7:

Answer to Question 7:

Question 8:

Answer to Question 8:

Other Notes:

GROUP CARINE'S INTERVIEW QUESTIONS TO ASK BILLIE *Into the Wild*

Question 1:

Question 2:

Question 3:

Question 4:

Question 5:

Question 6:

Question 7:

Question 8:

Other Notes:

INTERVIEW CHARACTER ROLE-PLAYING WORKSHEET: BILLIE *Into the Wild*

Group Billie

List Group Members:

Who will role-play Billie? _____

Who will role-play the investigative reporter for Walt? _____

Question 1:

Answer to Question 1:

Question 2:

Answer to Question 2:

Question 3:

Answer to Question 3:

Question 4:

Answer to Question 4:

Group Billie Worksheet Page 2
Question 5:

Answer to Question 5:

Question 6:

Answer to Question 6:

Question 7:

Answer to Question 7:

Question 8:

Answer to Question 8:

Other Notes:

GROUP BILLIE'S INTERVIEW QUESTIONS TO ASK WALT *Into the Wild*

Question 1:

Question 2:

Question 3:

Question 4:

Question 5:

Question 6:

Question 7:

Question 8:

Other Notes:

INTERVIEW CHARACTER ROLE-PLAYING WORKSHEET: WALT *Into the Wild*

Group Walt

List Group Members:

Who will role-play Walt? _____

Who will role-play the investigative reporter for Carine? _____

Question 1:

Answer to Question 1:

Question 2:

Answer to Question 2:

Question 3:

Answer to Question 3:

Question 4:

Answer to Question 4:

Group Walt Worksheet Page 2

Question 5:

Answer to Question 5:

Question 6:

Answer to Question 6:

Question 7:

Answer to Question 7:

Question 8:

Answer to Question 8:

Other Notes:

GROUP WALT'S INTERVIEW QUESTIONS TO ASK CARINE *Into the Wild*

Question 1:

Question 2:

Question 3:

Question 4:

Question 5:

Question 6:

Question 7:

Question 8:

Other Notes:

LESSON THIRTEEN

Objectives
1. To conduct oral interviews of Carine, Billie, and Walt
2. To practice "thinking on your feet" in the interviewing process
3. To explore the characters of Carine, Billie, and Walt in more depth
4. To exercise critical thinking skills

Activity #1
Use this class time to conduct the interviews of Carine, Billie, and Walt. After each interview is completed, ask the class to critique the quality of the questions and the effectiveness of the responses.

Activity #2
If class time remains after the interviews are conducted, introduce the Extra Discussion Questions to the class.

These questions can be used in a number of different ways, much like the study questions. Whether you have students prepare answers ahead of time in small groups or individually, or tackle them together as a whole class without pre-discussion work, these questions are meant as springboards to a deeper and more meaningful discussion than the study questions offer.

Depending on the level of your class, you may want to do all of the questions or skip some.

There is class time planned in the next meeting for more work on the discussion questions. You may want to have students prepare today for a discussion tomorrow.

LESSON FOURTEEN

Objectives
1. To discuss the book on a deeper than direct-recall level
2. To engage students' critical thinking skills
3. To look at the book as a whole in light of the elements of fiction, although it is actually a factual story
4. To practice forming and writing personal opinions
5. To express personal opinions about the book *Into the Wild*

Activity #1
Use this class time to complete the class discussions of the Extra Discussion Questions. The method by which this is done will depend on whether (or how) you had students prepare for the discussion. You may have individual or group reports, assign individual students to lead the discussions of particular questions, or hold a round-table discussion of each question.

Make sure students take or have notes answering all questions, as the questions will be used on the test.

Activity #2
Distribute Writing Assignment #3 and discuss the directions in detail. Give students the remainder of this class period to work on the assignment.

Be sure to give students a due date for this assignment.

EXTRA DISCUSSION QUESTIONS *Into the Wild*

Interpretive

1. At the beginning of this book, Chris McCandless is dead. What techniques of investigative reporting did Jon Krakauer use in piecing together this story?
2. The author visited bus 142 as part of his research for the book. How did he feel when he entered the bus for the first time?
3. Why was Jack London McCandless's favorite author?
4. In the author's opinion, what could Chris have done to save himself?
5. What impact did Chris have on Ron Franz even after Chris's death?
6. Although this is not a work of fiction, *Into the Wild* has the element of conflict. What conflicts are evident in this book? Is one conflict more dominant than the others?
7. Summarize Chris's character in a few sentences.
8. What do the quotations at the beginning of each part add to the book?

Critical

9. What aspects of Chris's character motivated others, like Jim Gallien, to care about him?
10. In what ways can Wayne Westerberg be considered to be a surrogate father for Chris?
11. Were McCandless's critics justified in describing him as unprepared and naive?
12. In what ways were the author and Chris alike as young men? How were they different?
13. Why was Chris drawn to menial work?
14. What is the author trying to say about McCandless by presenting brief biographies of Gene Rosellini, John Waterman, Carl McCunn, and Everett Ruess?
15. Which member of Chris's family had the closest relationship with Chris? Explain your answer.
16. Jon Krakauer is an investigative reporter. Characterize the style of this book. Is it an elaborate news report? A biography? A novel? What would you call it? Why?
17. In what ways has Mr. Krakauer influenced the reader's understanding of Chris McCandless and his story?
18. Look at the structure of the book and map its parts. Where is the climax of the book? Justify your answer.
19. Why did Chris McCandless go to Alaska, and why did he die there?
20. What universal themes are present in the story of Chris McCandless's life and death? Give examples of each.
21. Other than the obvious difference that this book is a true story, how is this work similar to and different from a work of fiction? If it were a fictitious story, how might it have been written differently? What elements of fiction are missing?
22. Most things the author writes are facts; however, he sometimes interjects his own opinions. Consider the section of the book that explores the exact cause of Chris's death. State which elements are fact and which are the author's opinions.
23. Consider where the author addresses whether or not Chris was suicidal. What facts does the author use to support his opinion that Chris was not suicidal?
24. To what conclusions does the author come about Chris's life and death? How does he arrive at each of these conclusions? State the main points of his evidence for each.

Critical/Personal Response

25. Compare Walt and Billie McCandless's relationships with Chris.
26. To what extent was Chris's decision to live alone in the Alaskan wilderness an expression of his idealistic view of nature?

27. Does Chris mature or grow as a person in the sixteen weeks he is alone in the Alaskan wilderness? If so, how? If not, why not?
28. Compare the author and Carine McCandless. What life lessons did they learn as they matured that Chris may have discovered had he lived?
29. The author describes this book as a "meandering inquiry." In what sense does the format of this book mirror Chris's life?
30. Both Chris and the author were isolated from civilization for a prolonged period of time. Compare and contrast the way each dealt with his time alone.
31. Define materialism. Then, discuss Chris's relationship with money and possessions. At times, he was motivated to make money, and at other times, he was motivated to give his belongings away. Why do you think he behaved this way?
32. Some critics suggest that Chris must have been mentally ill. For what reasons do you agree or disagree with this assessment?
33. Do you believe that at some point a young person should separate from his or her childhood family and childhood trauma to take control and responsibility for his or her own life choices? Do you think Chris reached this point? Did the author?
34. How successful is Jon Krakauer's book at answering questions about Chris McCandless's life and death? Justify your answer.
35. Which of the other people in the book were most interesting to you--either people Chris met along the way or other adventurers the author described? Choose which other person or group of people was most interesting, and state why.

Personal Response

36. If you could talk to Chris, what questions might you ask him?
37. List several types of risky behavior a young person today might embrace. For what reasons might a young person engage in these behaviors? With so many possible risky life choices, why do you think Chris chose to live alone in the Alaskan wild?
38. Is it practical or desirable to impose the "ideal" onto or into "reality"? For example, how realistic is it to live off of the land in this day and age? Thoreau lived in his cabin in the woods, and others have gone in search of the ideal, natural life. Is there a balance necessary between the ideal and reality, or do most of us just settle for that which is practical and easy? Is that a good thing--or not?
39. If you could add a chapter to this book, what aspect of Chris's life or character would you like to explore further?
40. Do you believe that at some point a young person should separate from his/her childhood family and childhood trauma to take control and responsibility for his/her life choices? Do you think Chris reached this point? Did the author?
41. Some critics suggest that Chris must have been mentally ill. For what reasons do you agree or disagree with this assessment?
42. Would traveling around the country and living off of the land be something you would like to do? Why or why not?
43. For the most part, as far as we know, Chris kept his feelings about his parents to himself, growing in dissatisfaction to the point of never wanting to see them again. Was this a good thing to do, or should he have expressed his opinions more openly with his family?
44. How do you feel about Chris's death? Do you think it was a tragedy? Do you think he just got what he deserved? What do you think?
45. What do you think of Chris's family: Walt, Billie, and Carine? State what you think of each person in the family.
46. Would you recommend this book to a friend? Why or why not?

WRITING ASSIGNMENT #3 *Into the Wild*

PROMPT
As a newspaper critic, write a review of *Into the Wild* expressing your opinion of Krakauer's work.

PREWRITING
Consider the following questions as you think about the content of your review:
--Do you see anything positive in the author's decision to write a book about McCandless's tragic experience?
--What did you learn from studying this book that might be helpful to you in the future?
--Would you change anything about the way the story is presented in the book? What advice would you give the author about any future publications?
--Would you recommend this book to others?

DRAFTING
A book review begins with the title of the book followed by the author's name and the date of publication.
Into the Wild
by Jon Krakauer
First published 1996
Reviewed by:

The first paragraph of a book review usually includes a brief summary of the story and a statement of the critic's overall opinion of the book. Book reviews must be interesting. The first sentence should entice the reader to continue reading.

The following paragraphs provide details supporting your opinion. The final paragraph should briefly summarize your opinions and recommendations.

PROOFREADING
When you finish the rough draft of your review, ask a student who sits near you to read it. He or she should tell you if the review was interesting and factually accurate. Make any necessary corrections and do a final proofreading, checking your grammar, spelling, organization, and the clarity of your ideas.

LESSON FIFTEEN

Objectives
To review all of the vocabulary work done in this unit

Activity
Choose one (or more) of the vocabulary review activities listed below and spend your class period as directed in the activity. Some of the materials for these review activities are located in the Vocabulary Resource section of this unit.

VOCABULARY REVIEW ACTIVITIES

1. Divide your class into two teams and have an old-fashioned spelling or definition bee.

2. Give each of your students (or students in groups of two, three, or four) an *Into the Wild* Vocabulary Word Search Puzzle. The person (group) to find all of the vocabulary words in the puzzle first wins.

3. Give students an *Into the Wild* Vocabulary Word Search Puzzle without the word list. The person or group to find the most vocabulary words in the puzzle wins.

4. Use an *Into the Wild* Vocabulary Crossword Puzzle. Put the puzzle onto a transparency on the overhead projector (so everyone can see it), and do the puzzle together as a class.

5. Give students an *Into the Wild* Vocabulary Matching Worksheet to do.

6. Divide your class into two teams. Use *Into the Wild* vocabulary words with their letters jumbled as a word list. Student 1 from Team A faces off against Student 1 from Team B. You write the first jumbled word on the board. The first student (1A or 1B) to unscramble the word wins the chance for his or her team to score points. If 1A wins the jumble, go to student 2A and give him or her a definition. He or she must give you the correct spelling of the vocabulary word which fits that definition. If he or she does, Team A scores a point, and you give student 3A a definition for which you expect a correctly spelled matching vocabulary word. Continue giving Team A definitions until a team member makes an incorrect response. An incorrect response sends the game back to the jumbled-word face-off, this time with students 2A and 2B. Instead of repeating giving definitions to the first few students of each team, continue with the student after the one who gave the last incorrect response on the team. For example, if Team B wins the jumbled-word face-off, and student 5B gave the last incorrect answer for Team B, you would start this round of definition questions with student 6B, and so on. The team with the most points wins!

7. Have students write a story in which they correctly use as many vocabulary words as possible. Have students read their compositions orally! Post the most original compositions on your bulletin board.

LESSON SIXTEEN

Objectives
1. To review the themes of *Into the Wild*
2. To identify character traits
3. To study specific quotations from the book, looking for the significance of those passages

Activity

Review with the class the themes of the book as stated in the Author's Note:

I inevitably came to reflect on other, larger subjects as well: the grip wilderness has on the American imagination, the allure high-risk activities hold for young men of a certain mind, the complicated, highly charged bond that exists between fathers and sons.

Explain to the students that although these are the three major themes in the book, they are not the only themes. Students are not restricted to only these three themes when completing the worksheet.

Remind the class that books were so important to McCandless that he allotted precious space for them in his backpack. The quotations at the beginnings of the chapters are mostly excerpts from the literature McCandless valued. They also mirror the themes in the book.

Divide the class into groups. Pass out the Quotations Worksheet. Each group should study the quotations given and decide which theme(s) is best illustrated by the quote. In addition, note what each quote reveals about McCandless's life, character, or motivations.

Then, read the quotes aloud and ask each group to read their responses to be critiqued by the other groups. There are NO correct answers to this worksheet.

QUOTATIONS WORKSHEET *Into the Wild*

Read the following quotations and discuss what each reveals about McCandless's life and character. In addition, state a theme for this story suggested by each quotation.

1. There was a hint in it [the Alaskan wild] of laughter, but of a laughter more terrible than any sadness – a laughter that was mirthless as the smile of the Sphinx, a laughter cold as the frost and partaking of the grimness of infallibility. It was the masterful and incommunicable wisdom of eternity laughing at the futility of life and the effort of life. It was the Wild, the savage, frozen-hearted Northland Wild.   --Jack London, *White Fang*

McCandless's life/character:

Theme:

2. It should not be denied…that being footloose has always exhilarated us. It is associated in our minds with escape from history and oppression and law and irksome obligations, with absolute freedom, and the road has always led west. Wallace Stegner, *The American West as Living Space*

McCandless's life/character:

Theme:

3. To the desert go prophets and hermits; through deserts go pilgrims and exiles. Here the leaders of the great religions have sought the therapeutic and spiritual values of retreat, not to escape but to find reality. Paul Shepard, *Man in the Landscape: A Historic View of the Esthetics of Nature*

McCandless's life/character:

Theme:

4. No man ever followed his genius till it misled him. Though the result were bodily weakness, yet perhaps no one can say that the consequences were to be regretted, for these were a life in conformity to higher principles. Henry David Thoreau, *Walden, or Life in the Woods*

McCandless's life/character:

Theme:

5. It is true that many creative people fail to make mature personal relationships, and some are extremely isolated. It is also true that, in some instances, trauma, in the shape of early separation or bereavement, has steered the potentially creative person toward developing aspects of his personality which can find fulfillment in comparative isolation. Anthony Storr, *Solitude: A Return to the Self*

McCandless's life/character:

Theme:

6. As to when I shall visit civilization, it will not be soon, I think. I have not tired of the wilderness; rather I enjoy its beauty and the vagrant life I lead, more keenly all the time. Letter from Everett Ruess to his Brother, Waldo

McCandless's life/character:

Theme:

7. There was no one around, neither family nor people whose judgment you respected. At such a time you felt the need of committing yourself to something absolute--life or truth or beauty--of being ruled by it in place of the man-made rules that had been discarded. Boris Pasternak, *Doctor Zhivago*

McCandless's life/character:

Theme:

Quotations Worksheet *Into the Wild* Page 3

8. I believe that every man who has ever been earnest to preserve his higher or poetic faculties in the best condition has been particularly inclined to abstain from animal food, and from much food of any kind…Henry David Thoreau, *Walden, or Life in the Woods*

McCandless's life/character:

Theme:

9. The mountains are dead stone, the people
 Admire or hate their stature, their insolent quietness,
 The mountains are not softened or troubled
 And a few dead men's thoughts have the same temper.   --Robinson Jeffers, "Wise Men in Their Bad Hours."

McCandless's life/character:

Theme:

10. ...Climb if you will, but remember that courage and strength are nought without prudence, and that a momentary negligence may destroy the happiness of a lifetime. Do nothing in haste; look well to each step; and from the beginning think what may be the end. Edward Whymper, *Scrambles Amongst the Alps*

McCandless's life/character:

Theme:

LESSON SEVENTEEN

Objectives
1. To pull together the ideas and events discussed at various points throughout this unit
2. To review the material covered in this unit as a way of helping students to prepare for the test

Activity

Choose one of the review games/activities suggested below and spend your class time as directed there.

REVIEW GAMES/ACTIVITIES *Into The Wild*

1. **Create-A-Test.** Ask the class to make up a unit test for *Into the Wild*. The test should have four sections: matching, true/false, short answer, and essay. Students may use half the class period to make the test and then swap papers and use the other half of the class period to take a test a classmate has devised (open book). You may want to use the unit test included in this packet or take questions from the students' unit tests to formulate your own test.

2. **Tic-Tac-Toe.** Take half the class period for students to make up true and false questions (including the answers). Collect the papers and divide the class into two teams. Draw a big tic-tac-toe grid on the board. Make one team X and one team O. Ask questions to each side, giving each student one turn. If the question is answered correctly, that students' team's letter (X or O) is placed in the box. If the answer is incorrect, no letter is placed in the box. The object is to get three in a row like tic-tac-toe. You may want to keep track of the number of games won for each team.

3. **Question Bee.** Take half the class period for students to make up questions (true/false and short answer). Collect the questions. Divide the class into two teams. You'll alternate asking questions to individual members of teams A & B (like in a spelling bee). The question keeps going from A to B until it is correctly answered. Then a new question is asked. A correct answer does not allow the team to get another question. Correct answers are +2 points; incorrect answers are -1 point.

4. Have students pair up and **quiz** each other from their study guides and class notes.

5. Give students an *Into the Wild* **crossword puzzle** to complete.

6. **Play What's My Line?.** This is similar to the old television show. Students assume the roles of different characters from the book. One student gives clues to the class or to a panel of contestants. The contestants try to guess the identity of the guest. Students may enjoy assisting you in creating rules and procedures for the game.

7. **Jumble Letter Face-Off.** Divide your class into two teams. Use *Into the Wild* crossword words with their letters jumbled as a word list. Student 1 from Team A faces off against Student 1 from Team B. You write the first jumbled word on the board. The first student (1A or 1B) to unscramble the word wins the chance for his or her team to score points. If 1A wins the jumble, go to student 2A and give him or her a clue. He or she must give you the correct word which matches that clue. If he or she does, Team A scores a point, and you give student 3A a clue for which you expect another correct response. Continue giving Team A clues until a team member makes an incorrect response. An incorrect response sends the game back to the jumbled-word face-off, this time with students 2A and 2B. Instead of repeating giving clues to the first few students of each team, continue with the student after the one who gave the last incorrect response on the team. For example, if Team B wins the jumbled word face-off, and student 5B gave the last

incorrect answer for Team B, you would start this round of clue questions with student 6B, and so on. The team with the most points wins!

8. **Play Jeopardy.** Divide the class into two groups. Assign each group a category or section from the book and have them devise answers for that category or section. Play the game according to the television show procedures.

9. **Play Drawing in the Details.** This is similar to Pictionary. Divide students into teams. A student from one team draws a scene from the book. (You may want to specify the chapter or section.) Drawings should be kept simple, to keep the pace lively. Students in the opposing team locate the scene in their books and read it aloud. If they are incorrect, the illustrator's team has a chance to guess. Involve students in setting up a scoring system and any other necessary rules.

LESSON EIGHTEEN

Objectives
To evaluate students understanding of the material covered in this unit

Activity
Distribute the unit tests and discuss the directions in detail. Give students ample time to complete the tests and then collect them for grading.

NOTES ABOUT THE TESTS IN THIS UNIT:
There are five different unit tests which follow.

There are two short answer tests which are based primarily on facts from the book. The answer key for short answer unit test 1 follows the student test. The answer key for short answer test 2 follows the student short answer unit test 2.

For the vocabulary sections of the short answer tests, you should choose 10 of the vocabulary words from this unit, read them orally and have students write them down. Then, either have students write a definition or use the words in sentences.

There are two multiple choice unit tests with answer keys following the second multiple choice test.

There is one advanced short answer unit test. It is based on the extra discussion questions and quotations. There is no key for the short answer questions and quotations. The answers will be based on the discussions you have had during class.

UNIT TESTS

SHORT ANSWER UNIT TEST 1 – *Into the Wild*

I. Matching

____ 1. John Waterman   A. Mayor of Hippie Cove
____ 2. Loren Johnson   B. Taught McCandless leatherworking
____ 3. Duck Hunters   C. Perished due to a misused hand signal
____ 4. Ron Franz   D. Mentally ill mountaineer who kept a journal
____ 5. Everett Ruess   E. One of McCandless's mistakes
____ 6. Devils Thumb   F. McCandless's grandfather
____ 7. Alexander Supertramp   G. Discovered McCandless's body
____ 8. Teklanika River   H. Colorado mountain the author climbs
____ 9. The Slabs   I. McCandless's shelter
____ 10. Ken Thompson   J. Offered McCandless the use of an old trailer
____ 11. Bus 142   K. Artist who vanished at age 20 in 1934
____ 12. Gene Rosellini   L. Helped Chris to reach the Gulf of California
____ 13. Carl McCunn   M. Old navy air base
____ 14. Buckley   N. McCandless's dog
____ 15. Charlie   O. McCandless's alias

II. Short Answer

1. How did Gallien try to dissuade Alex from carrying out his plan to live alone in the Alaskan wilderness?

2. Why did Yutan Construction place three junked buses in the wilderness?

3. How did Westerberg try to help McCandless?

4. What did Chris do with the twenty-four thousand dollars in his savings account?

5. What special request did Ron Franz make that made McCandless uncomfortable?

Short Answer Unit Test 1 Page 2

6. List three ways John Waterman's life story differed from Chris McCandless's story.

7. Why did McCandless purchase an aluminum canoe?

8. What advice did Walt give Chris after learning his son was lost in the Mojave Desert? How did Chris react to his father's concern?

9. What assets did the author have with him when he departed Boulder to begin his journey to the Devils Thumb?

10. How did the people of Kito's Kave bar react to the news that the author had successfully climbed the Devils Thumb?

11. What was the subject of most of McCandless's journal entries?

12. McCandless might have been rescued if he had started a forest fire as a distress signal. Why, in his sister Carine's opinion, did McCandless fail to do this?

13. What was the last book McCandless read?

14. After visiting the site of their son's death, what did Billie and Walt leave behind in bus 142?

Into the Wild

III. Essay

Complete the following sentence, and write an essay to support it.

Chris McCandless died because _____.

Support your opinion with events from the book. Your first paragraph should state your position. Add a paragraph for each supporting event and a concluding paragraph summarizing your ideas.

Into the Wild

IV. Vocabulary
    A. Write the vocabulary words you are given. After writing them down, go back and write in their definitions.

Word	Definition
1	
2	
3	
4	
5	
6	
7	
8	
9	
10	

ANSWER KEY SHORT ANSWER UNIT TEST 1 – *Into the Wild*

I. Matching

D	1. John Waterman	A.	Mayor of Hippie Cove
F	2. Loren Johnson	B.	Taught McCandless leatherworking
L	3. Duck Hunters	C.	Perished due to a misused hand signal
B	4. Ron Franz	D.	Mentally ill mountaineer who kept a journal
K	5. Everett Ruess	E.	One of McCandless's mistakes
H	6. Devils Thumb	F.	McCandless's grandfather
O	7. Alexander Supertramp	G.	Discovered McCandless's body
E	8. Teklanika River	H.	Colorado mountain the author climbs
M	9. The Slabs	I.	McCandless's shelter
G	10. Ken Thompson	J.	Offered McCandless the use of an old trailer
I	11. Bus 142	K.	Artist who vanished at age 20 in 1934
A	12. Gene Rosellini	L.	Helped Chris to reach the Gulf of California
C	13. Carl McCunn	M.	Old navy air base
N	14. Buckley	N.	McCandless's dog
J	15. Charlie	O.	McCandless's alias

II. Short Answer

1. How did Gallien try to dissuade Alex from carrying out his plan to live alone in the Alaskan wilderness?
   Gallien warned Alex that hunting was not easy. He tried to scare Alex with bear stories and pointed out that Alex's gun was no defense against a bear. He offered to drive Alex to Anchorage and buy him decent gear.

2. Why did Yutan Construction place three junked buses in the wilderness?
   In 1961 Yutan Construction Company upgraded the Stampede Trail. The buses, outfitted with bunks and a stove, were placed in the wilderness to serve as housing for construction workers.

3. How did Westerberg try to help McCandless?
   Westerberg gave McCandless a place to stay for three days and offered him a job should McCandless return to Carthage one day.

4. What did Chris do with the twenty-four thousand dollars in his savings account?
   Chris donated the money to OXFAM America which was a nonprofit organization formed to fight hunger.

5. What special request did Ron Franz make that made McCandless uncomfortable?
   Franz asked McCandless if he could adopt him.

6. List three ways John Waterman's life story differed from Chris McCandless's story.
   Both young men were raised in the Washington D.C. area. In addition, they both had poor relationships with their fathers. Waterman and McCandless both embarked on risky adventures knowing that they may never return.

7. Why did McCandless purchase an aluminum canoe?
   McCandless decided to use the canoe to travel down the Colorado River to the Gulf of California.

8. What advice did Walt give Chris after learning his son was lost in the Mojave Desert? How did Chris react to his father's concern?
   Walt suggested that Chris should be careful and let his parents know his whereabouts. Chris was angered by this advice. He thought his parents were idiots to worry about him.

9. What assets did the author have with him when he departed Boulder to begin his journey to the Devils Thumb?
   He had a 1960 Pontiac Star Chief and two hundred dollars.

10. How did the people of Kito's Kave bar react to the news that the author had successfully climbed the Devils Thumb?
    They were not surprised or impressed. Mostly they did not care.

11. What was the subject of most of McCandless's journal entries?
    Mostly McCandless wrote about food.

12. McCandless might have been rescued if he had started a forest fire as a distress signal. Why, in his sister Carine's opinion, did McCandless fail to do this?
    Carine believed that her brother would never burn a forest, even to save his own life.

13. What was the last book McCandless read?
    The last book McCandless read was Doctor Zhivago.

14. After visiting the site of their son's death, what did Billie and Walt leave behind in bus 142?
    They left a small brass plaque, wild flowers, and an emergency kit with a note instructing anyone who found the bus to call his/her parents.

III. Essay
Write an essay to support or refute the following statement:
   Chris McCandless died because he was inadequately prepared to survive in the Alaskan wilderness.

Support your opinion with events from the book. Your first paragraph should state your position. Add a paragraph for each supporting event and a concluding paragraph summarizing your ideas.

Evaluate the essay question according to your own criteria based on your expectations for your students.

IV. Vocabulary
   Write the vocabulary words and definitions you will use for this test.

Word	Definition
1	
2	
3	
4	
5	
6	
7	
8	
9	
10	

SHORT ANSWER UNIT TEST 2 – *Into the Wild*

Matching Unit Test 2 – *Into the Wild*

____ 1. Alexander Supertramp   A. Mayor of Hippie Cove
____ 2. Ken Thompson   B. Taught McCandless leatherworking
____ 3. Charlie   C. Perished due to a misused hand signal
____ 4. The Slabs   D. Mentally ill mountaineer who kept a journal
____ 5. Ron Franz   E. One of McCandless's mistakes
____ 6. Gene Rosellini   F. McCandless's grandfather
____ 7. John Waterman   G. Discovered McCandless's body
____ 8. Carl McCunn   H. Colorado mountain the author climbs
____ 9. Everett Ruess   I. McCandless's shelter
____ 10. Loren Johnson   J. Offered McCandless the use of an old trailer
____ 11. Buckley   K. Artist who vanished at age 20 in 1934
____ 12. Devils Thumb   L. Helped Chris reach the Gulf of California
____ 13. Teklanika River   M. Old navy air base
____ 14. Bus 142   N. McCandless's dog
____ 15. Duck Hunters   O. McCandless's alias

Short Answer Unit Test 2 – *Into the Wild*

1. List the supplies Alex carried into the Alaskan wild. Why did Gallien believe these supplies were inadequate?

2. How did Westerberg help the authorities locate McCandless's family?

3. For what reasons did Westerberg describe McCandless as both ethical and intelligent?

4. What did McCandless do with the twenty-four thousand dollars in his savings account?

5. Why did McCandless abandon his Datsun?

Short Answer Unit Test 2 *Into the Wild* Page 2

6. Where did McCandless work while staying in Bullhead City?

7. How was the Salton Sea created?

8. What advice did McCandless give Ron Franz in his letter?

9. Why did the monks (*papar*) risk their lives to cross the ocean from Ireland to Iceland?

10. Describe an event from Chris's high school years that illustrates his determination to follow his own path.

11. List three social issues Chris was passionate about in high school.

12. Why did Billie McCandless describe her son as "an entrepreneur"?

13. What did Chris do the summer between his freshman and sophomore years at Emory that helped his parents?

14. What was the purpose of the pair of aluminum curtain rods the author carried with him on his trek to the Devils Thumb?

III. Essay

One of the reasons the author wrote this book is because he "was haunted by the particulars of the boy's starvation and by vague, unsettling parallels between events in his life and those in my own."

Write a composition discussing the parallels between the author's life and Chris's life. Note: First, make a list of the ways both lives are similar. Then, write an introductory paragraph briefly describing them. Write a supporting paragraph for each similarity you introduce. Finally, write a concluding paragraph summarizing your ideas.

IV. Vocabulary
   A. Write the vocabulary words you are given. After writing them down, go back and write in their definitions.

Word	Definition
1	
2	
3	
4	
5	
6	
7	
8	
9	
10	

ANSWER KEY SHORT ANSWER UNIT TEST 2 – *Into the Wild*

I. Matching

O	1. Alexander Supertramp	A.	Mayor of Hippie Cove
G	2. Ken Thompson	B.	Taught McCandless leatherworking
J	3. Charlie	C.	Perished due to a misused hand signal
M	4. The Slabs	D.	Mentally ill mountaineer who kept a journal
B	5. Ron Franz	E.	One of McCandless's mistakes
A	6. Gene Rosellini	F.	McCandless's grandfather
D	7. John Waterman	G.	Discovered McCandless's body
C	8. Carl McCunn	H.	Colorado mountain the author climbs
K	9. Everett Ruess	I.	McCandless's shelter
F	10. Loren Johnson	J.	Offered McCandless the use of an old trailer
N	11. Buckley	K.	Artist who vanished at age 20 in 1934
H	12. Devils Thumb	L.	Helped Chris reach the Gulf of California
E	13. Teklanika River	M.	Old navy air base
I	14. Bus 142	N.	McCandless's dog
L	15. Duck Hunters	O.	McCandless's alias

II. Short Answer

1. List the supplies Alex carried into the Alaskan wild. Why did Gallien believe these supplies were inadequate?
   The only food Alex was carrying was a ten-pound bag of rice. His .22 caliber rifle was too small to kill large game. Alex's hiking boots were not waterproof. He had no ax, no snowshoes and no bug dope. Alex had a road map, but no compass. Alex also had a small camera in his backpack. Gallien used this camera to snap a photo of Alex.

2. How did Westerberg help the authorities locate McCandless's family?
   Westerberg heard a Paul Harvey radio broadcast about the unknown hiker. Westerberg believed the hiker could be Chris, so he phoned the Alaska State Troopers. Westerberg had McCandless's correct social security number from a W-4 form McCandless completed when he worked for Westerberg. With this information the authorities located Chris' half-brother, Sam.

3. For what reasons did Westerberg describe McCandless as both ethical and intelligent?
   Westerberg described McCandless as ethical because he never quit in the middle of a job. Westerberg considered McCandless intelligent because McCandless read a lot, used big words and thought deeply trying "to make sense of the world".

4. What did McCandless do with the twenty-four thousand dollars in his savings account?
   Chris donated the money to OXFAM America which was a nonprofit organization formed to fight hunger.

5. Why did McCandless abandon his Datsun?
   The Datsun was damaged in a flash flood. McCandless drained the battery trying to get it started so he wrote a note giving the car to anyone who was capable of getting the car out of the backcountry.

6. Where did McCandless work while staying in Bullhead City?
   McCandless worked at McDonald's.

7. How was the Salton Sea created?
   The Salton Sea was a small ocean created in 1905 from an engineering mistake. The plan was to dig a canal from the Colorado River to irrigate farmland in the Imperial Valley. Overflow from the river traveled into the newly dug canal and into the Salton sink. The water covered four hundred miles of desert.

8. What advice did McCandless give Ron Franz in his letter?
   McCandless advised Franz to leave Salton City and to lead a nomadic life.

9. Why did the monks (*papar*) risk their lives to cross the ocean from Ireland to Iceland?
   The monks were searching for "lonely places" away from civilization where they could dwell free of the "temptations of the world".

10. Describe an event from Chris's high school years that illustrates his determination to follow his own path.
    Chris received a failing grade on his lab reports even though he correctly completed the work because he refused to write the reports in the teacher's prescribed format.

11. List three social issues Chris was passionate about in high school.
    McCandless felt passionate about race issues, including apartheid in South Africa, the plight of the homeless and the need to eliminate hunger in this country.

12. Why did Billie McCandless describe her son as "an entrepreneur"?
    Chris excelled at making money. At age eight he successfully sold vegetables to the neighbors. He ran his own copy business at age twelve. In high school Chris was a top door-to-door salesman for a local contractor.

13. What did Chris do the summer between his freshman and sophomore years at Emory that helped his parents?
    Chris worked at his parent's business writing computer software.

14. What was the purpose of the pair of aluminum curtain rods the author carried with him on his trek to the Devils Thumb?
    The author tied the rods together to form a cross. He then strapped the cross to his backpack so that the rods extended away from his body. He hoped the curtain rods would span the width of any hidden crevasses he might accidentally uncover and in that way prevent him from slipping into the unknown depths of the glacier ice.

III. Essay
Write a composition discussing the parallels between the author's life and Chris's life.

Answers will vary. Evaluate students' work using your own criteria.

IV. Vocabulary

Write the vocabulary words and definitions you will use for this test.

Word	Definition
1	
2	
3	
4	
5	
6	
7	
8	
9	
10	

ADVANCED SHORT ANSWER UNIT TEST – *Into the Wild*

I. Matching

____ 1. Teklanika River   A. Mayor of Hippie Cove
____ 2. Carl McCunn   B. Taught McCandless leatherworking
____ 3. Charlie   C. Perished due to a misused hand signal
____ 4. The Slabs   D. Mentally ill mountaineer who kept a journal
____ 5. Buckley   E. One of McCandless's mistakes
____ 6. Bus 142   F. McCandless's grandfather
____ 7. Gene Rosellini   G. Discovered McCandless's body
____ 8. John Waterman   H. Colorado mountain the author climbs
____ 9. Ron Franz   I. McCandless's shelter
____ 10. Ken Thompson   J. Offered McCandless the use of an old trailer
____ 11. Devils Thumb   K. Artist who vanished at age 20 in 1934
____ 12. Alexander Supertramp   L. Helped Chris to reach the Gulf of California
____ 13. Loren Johnson   M. Old navy air base
____ 14. Everett Ruess   N. McCandless's dog
____ 15. Duck Hunters   O. McCandless's alias

II. Short Answer

1. Why was Jack London one of Chris's favorite authors?

2. What aspects of Chris's character motivated others to care about him?

3. Describe Chris's relationship with money and possessions.

4. What are three universal themes present in Chris McCandless's story?

5. Explain why the quotations are used at the beginning of each part of the book.

Advanced Short Answer Unit Test *Into the Wild* Page 2

6. Describe Chris's relationship with his parents.

7. Compare John Waterman's life story with Chris's life story.

8. Describe Chris's relationship with Wayne Westerberg.

9. Describe Chris's relationship with his sister.

10. Why did Chris go to Alaska?

11. Why does the author talk about himself and other adventurers in the story?

12. What did the author learn about his adventure from the reaction of the people at Kito's Kave bar when they heard the news that the author had successfully climbed the Devils Thumb?

Into the Wild

III. Essay

In the Epilogue, Walt McCandless describes his feelings after visiting the site of his son's death.

This brief visit, he says, has given him a slightly better understanding of why his boy came into this country. There is much about Chris that still baffles him and always will, but now he is a little less baffled. And for that small solace he is grateful.

As the author Jon Krakauer, write a letter to Walt McCandless helping him to understand his son's motivations for risking his life to live alone in the Alaskan wilderness and how Chris's relationship with his father may have changed had Chris survived his adventure.

This letter must be based on events from the book. First, organize your ideas by listing the reasons Chris traveled to Alaska. Your introductory paragraph should explain the purpose of the letter. Then, write one paragraph for each point you are making about Chris's motivation(s). The concluding paragraph should summarize your ideas.

Into the Wild

IV. Quotations: Explain the importance and meaning of the following quotations:

1. It is true that many creative people fail to make mature personal relationships, and some are extremely isolated. It is also true that, in some instances, trauma, in the shape of early separation or bereavement, has steered the potentially creative person toward developing aspects of his personality which can find fulfillment in comparative isolation. Anthony Storr, *Solitude: A Return to the Self*

2. I believe that every man who has ever been earnest to preserve his higher or poetic faculties in the best condition has been particularly inclined to abstain from animal food, and from much food of any kind…Henry David Thoreau, *Walden, or Life in the Woods*

3. It should not be denied…that being footloose has always exhilarated us. It is associated in our minds with escape from history and oppression and law and irksome obligations, with absolute freedom, and the road has always led west. Wallace Stegner, *The American West As Living Space*

ANSWER KEY ADVANCED SHORT ANSWER UNIT TEST – *Into the Wild*

I. Matching

E	1. Teklanika River	A. Mayor of Hippie Cove
C	2. Carl McCunn	B. Taught McCandless leatherworking
J	3. Charlie	C. Perished due to a misused hand signal
M	4. The Slabs	D. Mentally ill mountaineer who kept a journal
N	5. Buckley	E. One of McCandless's mistakes
I	6. Bus 142	F. McCandless's grandfather
A	7. Gene Rosellini	G. Discovered McCandless's body
D	8. John Waterman	H. Colorado mountain the author climbs
B	9. Ron Franz	I. McCandless's shelter
G	10. Ken Thompson	J. Offered McCandless the use of an old trailer
H	11. Devils Thumb	K. Artist who vanished at age 20 in 1934
O	12. Alexander Supertramp	L. Helped Chris to reach the Gulf of California
F	13. Loren Johnson	M. Old navy air base
K	14. Everett Ruess	N. McCandless's dog
L	15. Duck Hunters	O. McCandless's alias

Answers to the Short Answer, Essay, and Quotes sections will vary depending on your class discussions and the standard that you expect responses to meet.

MULTIPLE CHOICE UNIT TEST 1 – *Into the Wild*

I. Matching

____ 1. John Waterman   A. Mayor of Hippie Cove
____ 2. Loren Johnson   B. Taught McCandless leatherworking
____ 3. Duck Hunters   C. Perished due to a misused hand signal
____ 4. Ron Franz   D. Mentally ill mountaineer who kept a journal
____ 5. Everett Ruess   E. One of McCandless's mistakes
____ 6. Devils Thumb   F. McCandless's grandfather
____ 7. Alexander Supertramp   G. Discovered McCandless's body
____ 8. Teklanika River   H. Colorado mountain the author climbs
____ 9. The Slabs   I. McCandless's shelter
____ 10. Ken Thompson   J. Offered McCandless the use of an old trailer
____ 11. Bus 142   K. Artist who vanished at age 20 in 1934
____ 12. Gene Rosellini   L. Helped Chris to reach the Gulf of California
____ 13. Carl McCunn   M. Old navy air base
____ 14. Buckley   N. McCandless's dog
____ 15. Charlie   O. McCandless's alias

II. Multiple Choice

1. What alias did Chris McCandless use after he left home?
    a. Alex McCandless
    b. Alex Supertramp
    c. Chris Supertramp
    d. Mick McCandless

2. Which of the following items was McCandless carrying in his backpack as he entered the Alaskan bush?
    a. a compass
    b. bug dope
    c. several spiral notebooks
    d. a ten-pound bag of rice

3. After giving McCandless a ride to the Denali National Park, Jim Gallien tried to convince McCandless to abandon his plans to spend the summer alone in the Alaskan bush. Why was he unsuccessful?
    a. McCandless planned to purchase plenty of supplies before entering the Alaskan bush.
    b. McCandless knew his huge caliber rifle was sufficient protection against bears.
    c. McCandless was confident he had the necessary skills to survive.
    d. McCandless was suicidal and never planned to return from the bush.

4. Which one of the following items was found in bus 142 along with McCandless's body?
    a. a field guide to edible plants
    b. several spiral notebooks filled with McCandless's writing
    c. an ax
    d. a photograph of McCandless's family

Multiple Choice Unit Test 1 *Into The Wild* Page 2

5. Wayne Westerberg lived in
   a. Carthage, South Dakota.
   b. Oh-My-God Hot Springs, California
   c. Bullhead City, Arizona
   d. Fairbanks, Alaska

6. As a gesture of friendship, McCandless gave Westerberg
   a. a copy of Tolstoy's War and Peace.
   b. a copy of Jack London's Call of the Wild.
   c. a photograph of the two of them camping together.
   d. his rifle.

7. Which of the following statements about McCandless's family is NOT true?
   a. McCandless's father was an aerospace engineer.
   b. McCandless's parents gave him a 1982 Datsun as a gift when he graduated from Emory University.
   c. McCandless had six half-brothers and sisters from his father's first marriage.
   d. McCandless was close to his younger sister, Carine.

8. True or False: McCandless purchased an aluminum canoe to travel down the Colorado River to the Gulf of California.
   a. False
   b. True

9. Which of the following people wanted to adopt McCandless?
   a. Ron Franz
   b. Charlie
   c. Jan Burres
   d. Wayne Westerberg

10. True or False: McCandless's favorite author was Jack London.
    a. False
    b. True

11. What do Gene Rosellini, Carl McCunn and Everett Ruess all have in common?
    a. All of these men met helped McCandless travel to Alaska.
    b. Like McCandless, all of these men died after embarking on a risky adventure.
    c. All three of these men tried to convince McCandless to abandon his plans to spend the summer alone in the Alaskan bush.
    d. They all went to school with McCandless.

Multiple Choice Unit Test 1 *Into The Wild* Page 3

12. How did the authorities locate McCandless's family?
    a. The body was badly decomposed and could only be identified from McCandless's dental records.
    b. His sister traveled to Alaska to identify the body.
    c. McCandless's wallet was found on the body.
    d. Westerberg, who knew McCandless's real name and social security number, recognized the description of McCandless on the radio. He contacted the authorities. Using his social security number the authorities found McCandless's half-brother, Sam.

13. The *New York Times* reported that McCandless died from
    a. starvation.
    b. prolonged exposure to cold weather.
    c. pneumonia.
    d. a bear attack.

14. Identify Loren Johnson.
    a. Loren was the McCandless's family dog.
    b. Loren Johnson was the hiker who found McCandless's body.
    c. Loren Johnson was McCandless's closest high school friend.
    d. Loren was McCandless's grandfather.

15. Which of the following social/political issues did McCandless feel strongly about during his high school years?
    a. the nuclear arms race
    b. global warming
    c. hunger in America
    d. abortion

16. What did McCandless do the summer between his junior and senior years at Emory?
    a. He ran his own copy business.
    b. He worked as a door-to-door salesman for a local contractor.
    c. He drove to Alaska.
    d. He gave swimming lessons at the local YMCA.

17. What family secret did McCandless uncover that greatly damaged his relationship with his parents?
    a. Billie was not his real mother.
    b. His parent's marriage was crumbling.
    c. His father spent time in jail for fraud.
    d. His father continued seeing his first wife after falling in love with Billie.

18. Where was the Devils Thumb located?
    a. Canada
    b. Colorado
    c. Arizona
    d. Alaska

19. Which of the following statements about the author's quest to climb the Devils Thumb is FALSE?
    a. The author was attacked by a bear on his second night in the wild.
    b. At the author's request a pilot dropped six cartons of supplies at the base of the Devils Thumb.
    c. The author accidently set his tent on fire.
    d. The author began his journey to the Devils Thumb with only two hundred dollars.

20. True or False: The author's father was a physician who was admitted to a psychiatric hospital.
    a. True
    b. False

21. Once the author reached the summit he
    a. took pictures to prove he was successful.
    b. placed a flag at the top.
    c. experienced a feeling of sadness because his father was not with him.
    d. constructed a small tent as protection against the fierce winds.

22. When the patrons of Kito's Kave learned that the author had successfully climbed the Devils Thumb they
    a. asked him if he called his parents.
    b. bought him several rounds of drinks.
    c. told him he was naïve and foolish to take such a big risk.
    d. did not care.

23. What two requests did Gaylord Stuckley ask of McCandless after he dropped him off at the University of Alaska campus?
    a. Stuckley asked McCandless for Jack London's book, *Call of the Wild*, and for his parent's home address.
    b. Stuckley asked McCandless to write to him when he returns from the wild, and he begged McCandless to call his parents.
    c. Stuckley wanted McCandless to send him a letter and a photo of a wild moose.
    d. Stuckley asked McCandless for twenty dollars and a cigarette.

24. What was the heaviest item in McCandless's backpack?
    a. writing tablets
    b. food
    c. warm clothing
    d. books

25. In the author's opinion, which of the following events significantly contributed McCandless's death?
    a. McCandless was unable to preserve the moose meat.
    b. The Alaskan summer was uncharacteristically cold and McCandless lacked proper warm attire.
    c. McCandless ran out of ammunition for his rifle.
    d. McCandless could not cross the swollen Teklanika River.

26. What topic did McCandless mostly write about in his journal entries?
    a. his father
    b. the weather
    c. food
    d. the beautiful Alaskan bush

27. In the author's opinion, what was McCandless's cause of death?
    a. McCandless starved to death after suffering an unknown injury that prevented him from hunting for food.
    b. McCandless died from swainsonine poisoning caused by eating moldy wild potato seeds.
    c. McCandless mistook the poisonous wild sweet pea plant for the edible wild potato.
    d. McCandless committed suicide.

28. True or False: The authorities believed McCandless vandalized several nearby cabins.
    a. False
    b. True

29. Which of the following items did the author NOT see when he visited bus 142?
    a. a suicide note
    b. animal bones
    c. a collection of McCandless's personal belongings, including a blue toothbrush
    d. the mattress where McCandless died

30. Which of the following characters never fully recovered from McCandless's death and sometimes awakened at night hearing him calling for help?
    a. Carine
    b. Billie
    c. Walt
    d. Ron Franz

Into the Wild

II. Essay

McCandless wrote the following notes while living in bus 142. Write an essay based on these four notes discussing what each note reveals about McCandless's life, death, or philosophy. Begin with an introductory paragraph. Write one paragraph using events from the book to discuss each of the four notes. Then, write a concluding paragraph summarizing your ideas.

- NATURE/PURITY
- HAPPINESS ONLY REAL WHEN SHARED
- EXTREMELY WEAK, FAULT OF POT. SEED. MUCH TROUBLE JUST TO STAND UP. --STARVING. GREAT JEOPARDY.
- I HAVE HAD A HAPPY LIFE AND THANK THE LORD, GOODBYE AND MAY GOD BLESS ALL!

Into the Wild

IV. Vocabulary

____ 1. ominous A. emotionally expressive
____ 2. contumacious B. someone who spies on another's personal life
____ 3. subcutaneous C. criticized; reproached
____ 4. emotive D. search for food or provisions
____ 5. upbraided E. a policy of racial segregation in South Africa
____ 6. forage F. threatening; foreboding
____ 7. denizens G. inconsistent
____ 8. eremitic H. fantastic images seen as if in a dream
____ 9. posthumously I. upper jaw of an animal
____ 10. paucity J. stubbornly disobedient
____ 11. apartheid K. berated; chewed-out
____ 12. anomalous L. citizens
____ 13. lambasted M. scarcity
____ 14. phantasmagoria N. walk; move from place to place
____ 15. ambulate O. published or done after a person's death
____ 16. calamitous P. abnormally low body temperature
____ 17. Rubicon Q. line or boundary that is irrevocable once it is crossed
____ 18. hypothermia R. disasterous
____ 19. maxillae S. under the skin
____ 20. voyeur T. hermit-like; solitary

MULTIPLE CHOICE UNIT TEST 2 – *Into the Wild*

I. Matching

____ 1. Teklanika River
____ 2. Carl McCunn
____ 3. Charlie
____ 4. The Slabs
____ 5. Buckley
____ 6. Bus 142
____ 7. Gene Rosellini
____ 8. John Waterman
____ 9. Ron Franz
____ 10. Ken Thompson
____ 11. Devils Thumb
____ 12. Alexander Supertramp
____ 13. Loren Johnson
____ 14. Everett Ruess
____ 15. Duck Hunters

A. Mayor of Hippie Cove
B. Taught McCandless leatherworking
C. Perished due to a misused hand signal
D. Mentally ill mountaineer who kept a journal
E. One of McCandless's mistakes
F. McCandless's grandfather
G. Discovered McCandless's body
H. Colorado mountain the author climbs
I. McCandless's shelter
J. Offered McCandless the use of an old trailer
K. Artist who vanished at age 20 in 1934
L. Helped Chris to reach the Gulf of California
M. Old navy air base
N. McCandless's dog
O. McCandless's alias

II. Multiple Choice

1. What alias did Chris McCandless use after he left home?
   a. Alex McCandless
   b. Chris Supertramp
   c. Alex Supertramp
   d. Mick McCandless

2. Which of the following items was McCandless carrying in his backpack as he entered the Alaskan bush?
   a. a compass
   b. bug dope
   c. a ten-pound bag of rice
   d. several spiral notebooks

3. After giving McCandless a ride to the Denali National Park, Jim Gallien tried to convince McCandless to abandon his plans to spend the summer alone in the Alaskan bush. Why was he unsuccessful?
   a. McCandless was confident he had the necessary skills to survive.
   b. McCandless knew his huge caliber rifle was sufficient protection against bears.
   c. McCandless planned to purchase plenty of supplies before entering the Alaskan bush.
   d. McCandless was suicidal and never planned to return from the bush.

4. Which one of the following items was found in bus 142 along with McCandless's body?
   a. a photograph of McCandless's family
   b. several spiral notebooks filled with McCandless's writing
   c. an ax
   d. a field guide to edible plants

Multiple Choice Unit Test 2 *Into the Wild* Page 2

5. Wayne Westerberg lived in
   a. Carthage, South Dakota.
   b. Oh-My-God Hot Springs, California.
   c. Bullhead City, Arizona.
   d. Fairbanks, Alaska.

6. As a gesture of friendship, McCandless gave Westerberg
   a. his rifle.
   b. a copy of Jack London's Call of the Wild.
   c. a photograph of the two of them camping together.
   d. a copy of Tolstoy's War and Peace.

7. Which of the following statements about McCandless's family is NOT true?
   a. McCandless's parents gave him a 1982 Datsun as a gift when he graduated from Emory University.
   b. McCandless's father was an aerospace engineer.
   c. McCandless had six half-brothers and sisters from his father's first marriage.
   d. McCandless was close to his younger sister, Carine.

8. True or False: McCandless purchased an aluminum canoe to travel down the Colorado River to the Gulf of California.
   a. False
   b. True

9. Which of the following people wanted to adopt McCandless?
   a. Wayne Westerberg
   b. Charlie
   c. Jan Burres
   d. Ron Franz

10. True or False: McCandless's favorite author was Jack London.
    a. False
    b. True

11. What do Gene Rosellini, Carl McCunn and Everett Ruess all have in common?
    a. All of these men met helped McCandless travel to Alaska.
    b. All three of these men tried to convince McCandless to abandon his plans to spend the summer alone in the Alaskan bush.
    c. Like McCandless, all of these men died after embarking on a risky adventure.
    d. They all went to school with McCandless.

Multiple Choice Unit Test 2 *Into the Wild* Page 3

12. How did the authorities locate McCandless's family?
    a. The body was badly decomposed and could only be identified from McCandless's dental records.
    b. Westerberg, who knew McCandless's real name and social security number, recognized the description of McCandless on the radio. He contacted the authorities. Using his social security number the authorities found McCandless's half-brother, Sam.
    c. McCandless's wallet was found on the body.
    d. His sister traveled to Alaska to identify the body.

13. The *New York Times* reported that McCandless died from
    a. pneumonia.
    b. prolonged exposure to cold weather.
    c. starvation.
    d. a bear attack.

14. Identify Loren Johnson.
    a. Loren was McCandless's grandfather.
    b. Loren Johnson was the hiker who found McCandless's body.
    c. Loren Johnson was McCandless's closest high school friend.
    d. Loren was the McCandless's family dog.

15. Which of the following social/political issues did McCandless feel strongly about during his high school years?
    a. the nuclear arms race
    b. global warming
    c. abortion
    d. hunger in America

16. What did McCandless do the summer between his junior and senior years at Emory?
    a. He ran his own copy business.
    b. He drove to Alaska.
    c. He worked as a door-to-door salesman for a local contractor.
    d. He gave swimming lessons at the local YMCA.

17. What family secret did McCandless uncover that greatly damaged his relationship with his parents?
    a. His father continued seeing his first wife after falling in love with Billie.
    b. His parent's marriage was crumbling.
    c. His father spent time in jail for fraud.
    d. Billie was not his real mother.

18. Where was the Devils Thumb located?
    a. Canada
    b. Alaska
    c. Arizona
    d. Colorado

19. Which of the following statements about the author's quest to climb the Devils Thumb is FALSE?
    a. The author accidently set his tent on fire.
    b. At the author's request a pilot dropped six cartons of supplies at the base of the Devils Thumb.
    c. The author was attacked by a bear on his second night in the wild.
    d. The author began his journey to the Devils Thumb with only two hundred dollars.

20. True or False: The author's father was a physician who was admitted to a psychiatric hospital.
    a. False
    b. True

21. Once the author reached the summit he
    a. experienced a feeling of sadness because his father was not with him.
    b. placed a flag at the top.
    c. took pictures to prove he was successful.
    d. constructed a small tent as protection against the fierce winds.

22. When the patrons of Kito's Kave learned that the author had successfully climbed the Devils Thumb they
    a. asked him if he called his parents.
    b. did not care.
    c. told him he was naïve and foolish to take such a big risk.
    d. bought him several rounds of drinks.

23. What two requests did Gaylord Stuckley ask of McCandless after he dropped him off at the University of Alaska campus?
    a. Stuckley asked McCandless to write to him when he returns from the wild, and he begged McCandless to call his parents.
    b. Stuckley asked McCandless for Jack London's book, *Call of the Wild*, and for his parent's home address.
    c. Stuckley wanted McCandless to send him a letter and a photo of a wild moose.
    d. Stuckley asked McCandless for twenty dollars and a cigarette.

24. What was the heaviest item in McCandless's backpack?
    a. books
    b. food
    c. warm clothing
    d. writing tablets

25. In the author's opinion, which of the following events significantly contributed McCandless's death?
    a. McCandless was unable to preserve the moose meat.
    b. The Alaskan summer was uncharacteristically cold and McCandless lacked proper warm attire.
    c. McCandless could not cross the swollen Teklanika River.
    d. McCandless ran out of ammunition for his rifle.

26. What topic did McCandless mostly write about in his journal entries?
    a. his father
    b. the weather
    c. the beautiful Alaskan bush
    d. food

27. In the author's opinion, what was McCandless's cause of death?
    a. McCandless starved to death after suffering an unknown injury that prevented him from hunting for food.
    b. McCandless committed suicide.
    c. McCandless mistook the poisonous wild sweet pea plant for the edible wild potato.
    d. McCandless died from swainsonine poisoning caused by eating moldy wild potato seeds.

28. True or False: The authorities believed McCandless vandalized several nearby cabins.
    a. False
    b. True

29. Which of the following items did the author NOT see when he visited bus 142?
    a. a collection of McCandless's personal belongings, including a blue toothbrush
    b. animal bones
    c. a suicide note
    d. the mattress where McCandless died

30. Which of the following characters never fully recovered from McCandless's death and sometimes awakened at night hearing him calling for help?
    a. Walt
    b. Carine
    c. Billie
    d. Ron Franz

Into the Wild

III. Essay

In the Author's Note, Krakauer writes:
I interrupt [McCandless's] story with fragments of a narrative drawn from my own youth. I do so in the hope that my experiences will throw some oblique light on the enigma of Chris McCandless.

Write an essay discussing the ways you believe the author succeeded in explaining Chris McCandless's life choices through relating his own youthful experiences. Include at least three events from the author's life that shed some light for you on Chris McCandless's life.

IV. Vocabulary

____ 1. renunciation   A. lack of; shortage
____ 2. subcutaneous   B. abundance; plenty
____ 3. elasticity   C. intimidated; bullied
____ 4. upbraided   D. under the skin
____ 5. perfunctory   E. superficial; lacking enthusiasm
____ 6. lumpen   F. dominating; bossy; dictatorial
____ 7. inundating   G. published or done after a person's death
____ 8. opprobrium   H. formal letter
____ 9. epistle   I. flooding; covering
____ 10. posthumously   J. unplanned; impromptu
____ 11. veracity   K. of the lower class of society
____ 12. choler   L. criticism; judgment
____ 13. extemporaneous   M. criticized; reproached
____ 14. dearth   N. reproached; rebuked
____ 15. autocratic   O. incongruous; abnormal; out of context
____ 16. hectored   P. turning away from; self-denial
____ 17. Rubicon   Q. ability to be stretched out of shape and readily return to original form
____ 18. castigated   R. truth
____ 19. munificence   S. line or boundary that is irrevocable once it is crossed
____ 20. anomalous   T. anger

ANSWER KEYS MULTIPLE CHOICE UNIT TESTS *Into the Wild*

Matching	Test 1	Test 2
1	D	E
2	F	C
3	L	J
4	B	M
5	K	N
6	H	I
7	O	A
8	E	D
9	M	B
10	G	G
11	I	H
12	A	O
13	C	F
14	N	K
15	J	L

ANSWER KEY MULTIPLE CHOICE UNIT TESTS *Into the Wild*

Mult Choice	Test 1	Test 2
1	B	C
2	D	C
3	C	A
4	A	D
5	A	A
6	A	D
7	B	A
8	B	B
9	A	D
10	B	B
11	B	C
12	D	B
13	A	C
14	D	A
15	C	D
16	C	B
17	D	A
18	B	D
19	A	C
20	A	B
21	A	C
22	D	B
23	B	A
24	D	A
25	D	C
26	C	D
27	B	D
28	A	A
29	A	C
30	A	B

ANSWER KEY MULTIPLE CHOICE UNIT TESTS *Into the Wild*

Vocabulary	Test 1	Test 2
1	F	P
2	J	D
3	S	Q
4	A	M
5	C	E
6	D	K
7	L	I
8	T	L
9	O	H
10	M	G
11	E	R
12	G	T
13	K	J
14	H	A
15	N	F
16	R	C
17	Q	S
18	P	N
19	I	B
20	B	O

UNIT RESOURCE MATERIALS

BULLETIN BOARD IDEAS *Into the Wild*

1. For an advanced class, place the definitions of the following terms on the bulletin board under the title of the book. Leave space to add events from the story that illustrate each of these philosophical ideas: Idealism, Asceticism, Tolstoyan, and Transcendentalism.

2. Obtain movie posters from *Into the Wild* and post them on the bulletin board. Use them as visual aides when introducing the book.

3. Write several of the most significant quotations from the book on brightly colored paper and post them on the bulletin board. Use the quotes as discussion points after the book has been read.

4. Make a bulletin board relating to survival skills and equipment.

5. Have students bring in articles about young people who have engaged in risky behavior. Post these on the bulletin board, and discuss each one's merits and pitfalls.

6. Save a portion of your bulletin board for students' best *Into the Wild* writing assignments.

7. Make a bulletin board showcasing each of the books McCandless considered to be worth carrying with him into the wilderness. Leave room for students to add the titles of books they would consider to be essential. Use this board as a discussion point during the unit.

8. This book is rich in vocabulary relating to local color and mountain climbing. Make a bulletin board listing these words. As you complete sections of the book and discuss the vocabulary for each section, write the definitions on the bulletin board.

RELATED TOPICS *Into the Wild*

1. Survival Skills
2. Living a Natural Life in Modern Times
3. Famous Mountain Climbers
4. Mountain Climbing
5. River Canoeing
6. Tolstoy
7. Thoreau
8. Keeping a Diary
9. Photographic Journalism
10. Careers in the National Park Service
11. Denali National Park
12. Hunting in Alaska
13. Fishing Techniques
14. Edible Wild Plants
15. Wilderness Navigation
16. Native People of Alaska
17. Transcendentalism
18. Parent-Teen Relations
19. Emory University

MORE ACTIVITIES *Into the Wild*

1. Have students design a new book cover (front, back, and inside flaps) for *Into the Wild*.
2. Have students select a character from the book and complete the "I Am" poem from that character's point of view. (See the following handout.)
3. After completing the reading of the book, take a class period to revisit the quotes at the beginning of each chapter. Assign each student or small groups of students one of the chapter introductions. Students should consider the quote and then explain its significance in relation to the content of the chapter it heads. Give students ample time to thoughtfully consider the quotes, then come together as a class to discuss each one.
4. With the class, plot the events of the story on a storyline or storyboard. After doing so, tell students to consider each point along the way and find places where "if only" Chris had done something different, he might have had a much different ending. Discuss what he could have done differently that would have had a positive impact on the outcome.
5. Together with the class, make a chart of the adventurous characters in the book, their personal traits, the main things they did, and the outcomes. Put the names of the characters in the left-hand column and make columns to the right of that for each of the other information categories. Discuss the similarities and differences among the adventurers.
6. Explore the Native Americans of Alaska with your class. There are many online resources about the native tribes of Alaska: the Inupiaq, Yupik, Aleut, Eyak, Tlingit, Haida, Tsimshian, and others. Either as a group or an individual project, have students find out more about these interesting people and cultures.
7. The Related Topics list in this unit provides interesting topics related to the events, themes, and places in this book. It can be used as a springboard for project or research ideas.
8. Have the students read a related book (fiction or nonfiction) and write a brief book review summarizing the story and explaining how it related to *Into the Wild*. It is a good idea to keep related books in the classroom for students who finish early. Jack London books or other titles by Jon Krakauer would be good choices.
9. Ask the students to expand one of McCandless's journal entries.
10. The night before class, have students remove everything but five items from their book bags/back packs. Purses must be left at home, and pockets must be empty. They must then survive the entire day in school with only those five items. Students must not borrow equipment, food, paper, cosmetics, etc. from others. Then, write a journal entry based on this experience.
11. Divide the class into two groups for a debate on whether or not McCandless was sufficiently prepared for his Alaskan adventure.
12. Twenty years after her brother's death, Carine McCandless maintains a website with information related to Chris and *Into the Wild*. Find this website and review its content. Write a letter to Carine, 20 years after Chris's death, letting her know what you learned from Chris's story.

"I Am" Poem

Complete this "I am" poem. You may select any character from the book to do this poem about. Be sure to write from his or her point of view and think about the things he or she would feel. You may use some short one word answers, but do not make each line only a few words. You should try to provide support from the novel to really develop this poem so that it reveals information and insight about the character you select.

I am (2 characteristics your character has)
I wonder (something your character wonders)
I hear (something real or imaginary your character hears)
I see (something real or imaginary your character sees)
I want (something your character desires)
I am (the first line of the poem repeated)

I pretend (something your character pretends to do)
I feel (something real or imaginary your character feels emotionally)
I touch (something real or imaginary your character would touch physically)
I worry (something your character worries about)
I cry (something that makes your character upset)
I am (the first line of the poem repeated)

I understand (something your character knows)
I say (something your character believes in)
I dream (something your character would dream about)
I try (something your character makes an effort to do)
I hope (something your character hopes for)
I am (the first line of the poem repeated)

UNIT WORD LIST *Into the Wild*

No.	Word	Clue/Definition
1.	ABANDONED	Chris did this to his car.
2.	ALEX	Chris's alias
3.	APARTHEID	African social issue Chris was passionate about
4.	ATHIEST	Franz became one after he learned of Chris's death.
5.	BELT	It had a pictorial record of Chris's adventures.
6.	BILLIE	Chris's mom
7.	BOOTS	Gallien gave these to Alex.
8.	BULLHEAD	Chris worked at McDonald's in this city.
9.	BUS	Chris's Alaskan base camp
10.	CAR	The graduation gift Chris refused
11.	CARINE	Chris's sister
12.	CARTHAGE	Westerberg's hometown
13.	CHARLIE	He let Chris stay at an old trailer.
14.	COMPLEXES	Charlie thought Chris was a nice guy with a lot of these.
15.	DATSUN	McCandless's beloved car
16.	EMORY	University Chris attended
17.	ETHICAL	Westerberg described Alex as this.
18.	FOOD	Subject of most of Chris's journal entries
19.	FRANZ	He wanted to adopt Chris.
20.	GALLIEN	He gave Alex a ride to Denali National Park
21.	GILLMER	Chris's closest friend in high school
22.	HAPPY	"I have had a ___ life."
23.	HUNDRED	Number of days Chris survived in the wild
24.	JAN	She sold knick-knacks.
25.	LEATHERWORKING	Skill Franz taught Chris
26.	LONDON	Chris's favorite author who wrote about Alaska
27.	LOREN	Adored grandfather who loved the outdoors
28.	MCCANDLESS	Chris
29.	MCCUNN	He used the wrong emergency signal.
30.	MONKS	They crossed the ocean to avoid worldly temptation.
31.	MOODY	Charlie described Chris as this.
32.	NASA	Walt worked for this agency.
33.	OUTSIDE	Magazine that printed Krakauer's first McCandless story
34.	PLASTIC	What Chris called his co-workers in Bullhead City
35.	RICE	Alex's packed food staple
36.	ROSELLINI	Mayor of Hippie Cove
37.	RUESS	Lan Rameau
38.	SALTON	Sea created by an engineering mistake

Unit Word List *Into the Wild* Page 2

No.	Word	Clue/Definition
39.	SAM	The first family member to learn of Chris's death
40.	SAVINGS	Chris donated his to charity.
41.	SEEDS	Contaminated food source from wild potatoes
42.	SLABS	Home for vagabonds
43.	STARVATION	Cause of Chris's death
44.	STIKINE	Ice Cap of Krakauer's adventure
45.	STUCKEY	He drove McCandless to Fairbanks.
46.	SUPERTRAMP	Alexander ____
47.	TEKLANIKA	River Chris could not cross
48.	TENT	Krakauer's caught on fire.
49.	THUMB	Devil's ____
50.	WALT	Chris's dad
51.	WATERMAN	Expert climber who spent time in a mental hospital
52.	WESTERBERG	He hired Chris to work at his grain elevators.
53.	ZHIVAGO	Last book McCandless read

WORD SEARCH *Into the Wild*

```
D C L C S E T H I C A L R R L C T P
P A W G S T W J F T A T A O L S H D
R N T M S F A H Y R S C R F E Z U A
S O Z S E W H R I X A E D S M Z M T
Y E K C U T S N V L N N U C C M B H
P W M W R N I A T A O B Z A D A O E
A A E L A L H F V D T V R C O P O I
S U B S L L N O N I R I E M N A T S
T M K E T A T O X E N N O O A R S T
T O S E J E L D M E I G E N L T U H
Y O W D R V R L R K T I S K D H G E
R D N S T I L B I S L A B S S E U M
T Y M N J I C T E L P E H O F I A O
F Z E F G C S E I R L X N Q B D W R
H T H A P P Y B H T G B U C K L E Y
```

Alex's packed food staple (4)
Cause of McCandless's death (10)
Charlie described Chris as this (5)
Chris ate these from wild potatoes. (5)
Chris donated this to charity (7)
Chris's adored grandfather who loved the outdoors (5)
Chris's dad (4)
Chris's favorite author who wrote about Alaska (6)
Chris's half-brother who was the first family to hear Chris died (3)
Chris's mom (6)
Chris's river transportation (5)
Chris's younger sister (6)
Closest friend of Chris in high school (7)
Devils ____ (5)
Drove McCandless to Fairbanks (7)
Franz became one after he learned of Chris's death. (7)
Gallien gave these to Alex. (5)
He used the wrong emergency hand signal. (6)
Hired Chris to work at his grain elevators (10)
Home for vagabonds (5)
I have had a ___ life. (5)

Ice Cap of Krakauer's adventure (7)
It had a pictorial record of Chris's adventures (4)
Jan's boyfriend (3)
Krakauer's caught on fire (4)
Lan Rameau (5)
Mayor of Hippie Cove (9)
McCandless family dog (7)
McCandless's beloved car (6)
Ms. Burris who sold knick-knacks (3)
Place of employment in Bullhead City (9)
Ron who wanted to adopt Chris (5)
Social issue Chris felt passionate about (9)
Subject of most of Chris's journal entries (4)
The refused graduation gift (3)
They crossed the ocean to find places away from the temptations of the world. (5)
They were placed in the wilderness as housing. (5)
University Chris attended (5)
Walt worked for this agency. (4)
Walt's ___ damaged his relationship with Chris (4)
Westerberg described Alex as this. (7)
When Chris's family became very worried (6)
___ 142; Chris's base camp (3)

ANSWER KEY WORD SEARCH *Into the Wild*

```
D C     S E T H I C A L   R L   T
  A     S T     F   A   A O   S H
  N T   S     A   R S C R   E   U A
    O   S E     R I   A E   S M   M T
Y E K C   U T S N V   N N U C C M B H
P W M W R N I A   A O B Z A D A O E
A A E   A L   F V D T   R   O P O I
S U B S L L N O N I R I E M N A T S
T M   E T A T O   E N N O O A R S T
  O S E J E L D M E I G E N L T U
    O   D R   R L   K   I S K D H G E
R D   S T I L B I S L A B S S E U M
    Y   N   I C T E L   E   O   I A O
        E   G   S E I R L       B D   R
  T H A P P Y B   T G B U C K L E Y
```

Alex's packed food staple (4)
Cause of McCandless's death (10)
Charlie described Chris as this (5)
Chris ate these from wild potatoes. (5)
Chris donated this to charity (7)
Chris's adored grandfather who loved the outdoors (5)
Chris's dad (4)
Chris's favorite author who wrote about Alaska (6)
Chris's half-brother who was the first family to hear Chris died (3)
Chris's mom (6)
Chris's river transportation (5)
Chris's younger sister (6)
Closest friend of Chris in high school (7)
Devils ____ (5)
Drove McCandless to Fairbanks (7)
Franz became one after he learned of Chris's death. (7)
Gallien gave these to Alex. (5)
He used the wrong emergency hand signal. (6)
Hired Chris to work at his grain elevators (10)
Home for vagabonds (5)
I have had a ____ life. (5)

Ice Cap of Krakauer's adventure (7)
It had a pictorial record of Chris's adventures (4)
Jan's boyfriend (3)
Krakauer's caught on fire (4)
Lan Rameau (5)
Mayor of Hippie Cove (9)
McCandless family dog (7)
McCandless's beloved car (6)
Ms. Burris who sold knick-knacks (3)
Place of employment in Bullhead City (9)
Ron who wanted to adopt Chris (5)
Social issue Chris felt passionate about (9)
Subject of most of Chris's journal entries (4)
The refused graduation gift (3)
They crossed the ocean to find places away from the temptations of the world. (5)
They were placed in the wilderness as housing. (5)
University Chris attended (5)
Walt worked for this agency. (4)
Walt's ____ damaged his relationship with Chris (4)
Westerberg described Alex as this. (7)
When Chris's family became very worried (6)
____ 142; Chris's base camp (3)

CROSSWORD *Into the Wild*

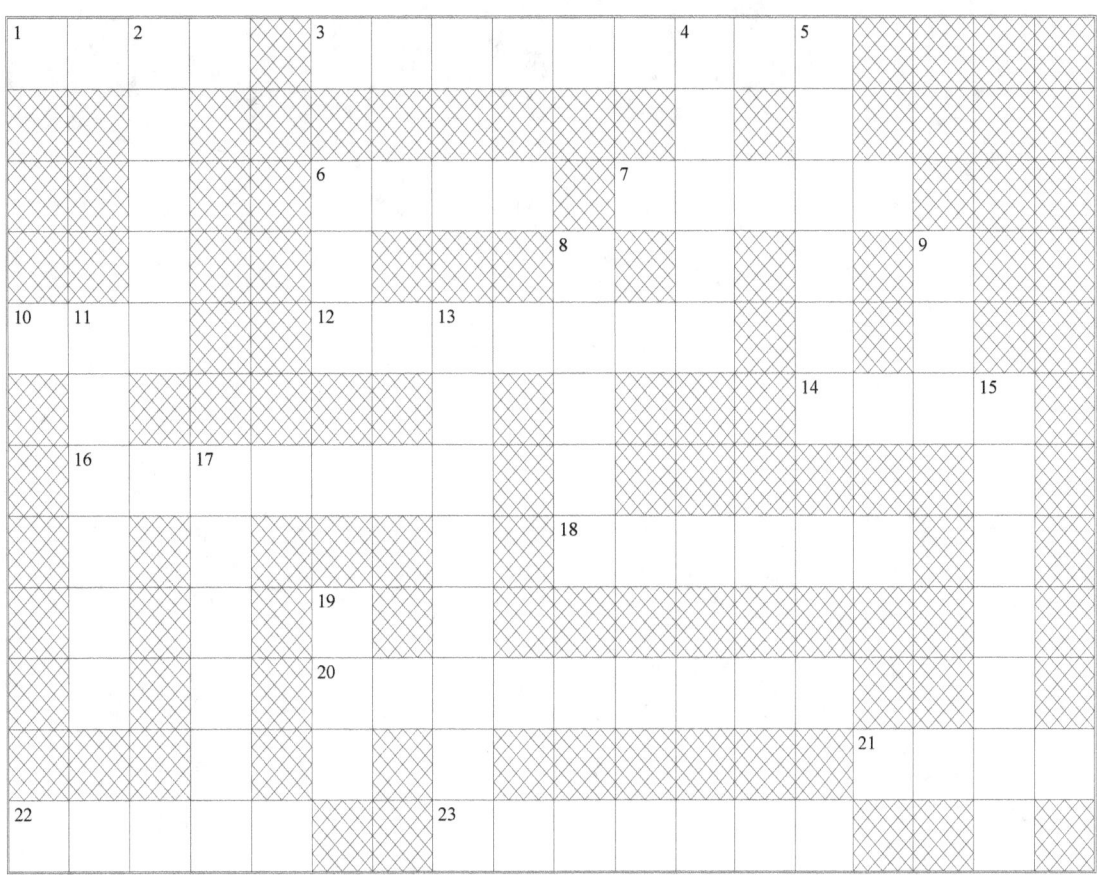

Across
1. Chris's dad
3. Social issue Chris felt passionate about
6. It had a pictorial record of Chris's adventures
7. Gallien gave these to Alex.
10. Ms. Burris who sold knick-knacks
12. McCandless family dog
14. Walt worked for this agency.
16. Closest friend of Chris in high school
18. Sea created by an engineering mistake
20. What happened to the car
21. Walt's ___ damaged his relationship with Chris
22. Ron who wanted to adopt Chris
23. Westerberg described Alex as this.

Down
2. Chris's adored grandfather who loved the outdoors
4. University Chris attended
5. McCandless's beloved car
6. Jan's boyfriend
8. Home for vagabonds
9. ___ 142; Chris's base camp
11. When Chris's family became very worried
13. Westerberg's hometown
15. Franz became one after he learned of Chris's death.
17. Chris's favorite author who wrote about Alaska
19. The refused graduation gift

ANSWER KEY CROSSWORD *Into the Wild*

	1 W	2 A	L	T		3 A	P	A	R	T	4 H	E	5 I	D		
		O									M		A			
		R				6 B	E	L	T		7 B	O	O	T	S	
		E				O			8 S		R		S		9 B	
10 J	11 A	N		12 B	U	C	K	L	E	Y		U		U		
	U				A		A					14 N	A	S	15 A	
	16 G	17 I	L	L	M	E	R		B						T	
	U		O				T		18 S	A	L	T	O	N	H	
	S		N		19 C		H								E	
	T		D		A	B	A	N	D	O	N	E	D		I	
			O		R		G					21 P	A	S	T	
22 F	R	A	N	Z		23 E	T	H	I	C	A	L			T	

Across
1. Chris's dad
3. Social issue Chris felt passionate about
6. It had a pictorial record of Chris's adventures
7. Gallien gave these to Alex.
10. Ms. Burris who sold knick-knacks
12. McCandless family dog
14. Walt worked for this agency.
16. Closest friend of Chris in high school
18. Sea created by an engineering mistake
20. What happened to the car
21. Walt's damaged his relationship with Chris
22. Ron who wanted to adopt Chris
23. Westerberg described Alex as this.

Down
2. Chris's adored grandfather who loved the outdoors
4. University Chris attended
5. McCandless's beloved car
6. Jan's boyfriend
8. Home for vagabonds
9. ___ 142; Chris's base camp
11. When Chris's family became very worried
13. Westerberg's hometown
15. Franz became one after he learned of Chris's death.
17. Chris's favorite author who wrote about Alaska
19. The refused graduation gift

MATCHING *Into the Wild*

_____ 1. EMORY   A. Sea created by an engineering mistake

_____ 2. ZHIVAGO   B. Alex's packed food staple

_____ 3. MCCUNN   C. Chris's half-brother who was the first family to hear Chris died

_____ 4. MONKS   D. Charlie thought Chris was a nice guy with a lot of ___.

_____ 5. WALT   E. Last book McCandless read

_____ 6. SALTON   F. Chris's dad

_____ 7. STUCKEY   G. He used the wrong emergency hand signal.

_____ 8. HUNDRED   H. Gave Alex a ride to Denali Nat'l Park

_____ 9. GALLIEN   I. Let Chris stay at an old trailer

_____ 10. OUTSIDE   J. Number of days Chris survived in the wild

_____ 11. APARTHEID   K. University Chris attended

_____ 12. COMPLEXES   L. Magazine with Krakauer's first McCandless story

_____ 13. WESTERBERG   M. I have had a ___ life.

_____ 14. SUPERTRAMP   N. It had a pictorial record of Chris's adventures

_____ 15. BUS   O. They crossed the ocean to find places away from the temptations of the world.

_____ 16. RICE   P. Hired Chris to work at his grain elevators

_____ 17. SAM   Q. Social issue Chris felt passionate about

_____ 18. CHARLIE   R. Alexander; Chris's alias

_____ 19. HAPPY   S. ___ 142; Chris's base camp

_____ 20. BELT   T. Drove McCandless to Fairbanks

ANSWER KEY MATCHING *Into the Wild*

K	1. EMORY	A. Sea created by an engineering mistake
E	2. ZHIVAGO	B. Alex's packed food staple
G	3. MCCUNN	C. Chris's half-brother who was the first family to hear Chris died
O	4. MONKS	D. Charlie thought Chris was a nice guy with a lot of ___.
F	5. WALT	E. Last book McCandless read
A	6. SALTON	F. Chris's dad
T	7. STUCKEY	G. He used the wrong emergency hand signal.
J	8. HUNDRED	H. Gave Alex a ride to Denali Nat'l Park
H	9. GALLIEN	I. Let Chris stay at an old trailer
L	10. OUTSIDE	J. Number of days Chris survived in the wild
Q	11. APARTHEID	K. University Chris attended
D	12. COMPLEXES	L. Magazine with Krakauer's first McCandless story
P	13. WESTERBERG	M. I have had a ___ life.
R	14. SUPERTRAMP	N. It had a pictorial record of Chris's adventures
S	15. BUS	O. They crossed the ocean to find places away from the temptations of the world.
B	16. RICE	P. Hired Chris to work at his grain elevators
C	17. SAM	Q. Social issue Chris felt passionate about
I	18. CHARLIE	R. Alexander; Chris's alias
M	19. HAPPY	S. ___ 142; Chris's base camp
N	20. BELT	T. Drove McCandless to Fairbanks

JUGGLE LETTERS *Into the Wild*

_____ = 1. ADIHEPTAR
   Social issue Chris felt passionate about

_____ = 2. SUB
   ___ 142; Chris's base camp

_____ = 3. CNMNUC
   He used the wrong emergency hand signal.

_____ = 4. ESOIUDT
   Magazine with Krakauer's first McCandless story

_____ = 5. VIAATTRNSO
   Cause of McCandless's death

_____ = 6. EMEOSXCLP
   Charlie thought Chris was a nice guy with a lot of ___.

_____ = 7. PATREMSRUP
   Alexander; Chris's alias

_____ = 8. NCIERA
   Chris's younger sister

_____ = 9. ATOSLN
   Sea created by an engineering mistake

_____ =10. ERSSU
   Lan Rameau

_____ =11. ELLIBI
   Chris's mom

_____ =12. ZGHAVOI
   Last book McCandless read

ANSWER KEY JUGGLE LETTERS *Into the Wild*

APARTHEID = 1. ADIHEPTAR
Social issue Chris felt passionate about

BUS = 2. SUB
___ 142; Chris's base camp

MCCUNN = 3. CNMNUC
He used the wrong emergency hand signal.

OUTSIDE = 4. ESOIUDT
Magazine with Krakauer's first McCandless story

STARVATION = 5. VIAATTRNSO
Cause of McCandless's death

COMPLEXES = 6. EMEOSXCLP
Charlie thought Chris was a nice guy with a lot of ___.

SUPERTRAMP = 7. PATREMSRUP
Alexander; Chris's alias

CARINE = 8. NCIERA
Chris's younger sister

SALTON = 9. ATOSLN
Sea created by an engineering mistake

RUESS =10. ERSSU
Lan Rameau

BILLIE =11. ELLIBI
Chris's mom

ZHIVAGO =12. ZGHAVOI
Last book McCandless read

VOCABULARY RESOURCE MATERIALS

Into the Wild Vocabulary

No.	Word	Clue/Definition
1.	AMBULATE	walk; move from place to place
2.	ANOMALY	irregularity; exception
3.	APARTHEID	a policy of racial segregation in South Africa
4.	APOLOGIA	defense of one's own actions
5.	ATHEIST	one who does not believe in God or any deity
6.	AUTOCRATIC	dominating; bossy; dictatorial
7.	AXIOMS	established truths, rules, or principles
8.	CALAMITOUS	disasterous
9.	CASTIGATED	reproached; rebuked
10.	CELIBATE	living without having sexual intercourse
11.	CHOLER	anger
12.	CONGRESS	the act of coming together
13.	CONTUMACIOUS	stubbornly disobedient
14.	CONVIVIAL	social; enjoying feasting together and good company
15.	COPIOUS	plentiful; abundant in number
16.	DEARTH	lack of; shortage
17.	DEMARCATES	distinguishes; sets apart
18.	DENIZENS	citizens
19.	DERELICT	abandoned
20.	EGRESS	means of exit; a way out
21.	ELASTICITY	ability to be stretched out of shape and readily returned to original form
22.	EMETIC	something that causes vomiting
23.	EMOTIVE	emotionally expressive
24.	ENIGMA	mystery; something difficult to understand
25.	EPIPHANY	sudden realization; illuminating discovery or understanding
26.	EPISTLE	formal letter
27.	EQUANIMITY	calmness; relaxed or balanced state of mind
28.	EREMETIC	hermit-like; solitary
29.	ETHICAL	conforming to standards of conduct
30.	EXCRETE	eliminate from blood, organs, or tissues
31.	EXTEMPORANEOUS	unplanned; impromptu
32.	FATUOUS	foolish; ridiculous
33.	FORAGE	search for food or provisions
34.	FULMINATED	actively criticized; ranted
35.	GAUNT	excessively thin
36.	HECTORED	intimidated; bullied
37.	HUBRIS	extreme or exaggerated self-confidence
38.	HYPOTHERMIA	abnormally low body temperature

Copyrighted

Vocabulary Word List *Into the Wild* Page 2

No.	Word	Clue/Definition
39.	IDIOSYNCRATIC	eccentric; peculiar
40.	INSIDUOUSLY	dangerously subtle; developing very slowly until it is too late
41.	INUNDATING	flooding; covering
42.	INVEIGLED	wangled; acquired through ingenuity
43.	LAMBASTED	berated; chewed-out
44.	LAMPOONED	satirized; ridiculed
45.	LENITY	leniency; acceptance; tolerance
46.	LUMPEN	of the lower class of society
47.	MADRIGAL	song with several unaccompanied voices singing in harmony
48.	MAXILLAE	upper jaw of an animal
49.	METASTASIZED	spread; grown
50.	MONOMAINA	excessive fixation on a single idea
51.	MUNIFICENCE	abundance; plenty
52.	NARCISSIST	self-absorbed person with an inflated self-image
53.	OMINOUS	threatening; foreboding
54.	ONEROUS	burdensome
55.	OPINED	remarked; commented, as in expressing an opinion criticism;
56.	OPPROBRIUM	judgment
57.	PANACHE	style; flamboyance
58.	PAUCITY	scarcity
59.	PELLUCID	translucently clear
60.	PEREGRINATIONS	travels
61.	PERFUNCTORY	superficial; lacking enthusiasm
62.	PHANTASMAGORIA	fantastic images seen as if in a dream
63.	PLEBEIAN	common or crude in manner
64.	PORTAGE	carry or transport a boat over land
65.	POSITED	strongly proposed or assumed; fixed
66.	POSTHUMOUSLY	published or done after a person's death
67.	PROGENY	offspring; children
68.	RECONDITE	difficult for ordinary people to understand; obscure
69.	RENUNCIATION	turning away from; self-denial
70.	RICTUS	open-mouthed grin
71.	RUBICON	line or boundary that is irrevocable once it is crossed
72.	SANCTIMONIOUS	falsely pious or devout
73.	SINEWY	stringy but strong
74.	SOBRIQUET	nickname
75.	SONOROUS	loud; impressive
76.	SUBCUTANEOUS	under the skin
77.	SURFEIT	excess
78.	UNALLOYED	unqualified; pure

No.	Word	Clue/Definition
79.	UNGULATE	animal with hooves
80.	UNHANDSELLED	unforgiving
81.	UPBRAIDED	criticized; reproached
82.	VAGARIES	uncertainties
83.	VERACITY	truthfulness; honesty
84.	VOLITION	determination; will
85.	VOYEUR	someone who spies on another's personal life

VOCABULARY WORD SEARCH *Into the Wild*

```
S O N O R O U S I N V E I G L E D Q
I D E R O T C E H T E U Q I R B O S
E N U P B R A I D E D Z A Q U D E K
V N U L M F L R N E P M U L B E G Y
O O I N R H A A L E N I T Y I Y A K
Z M Y G D L M G Z Q D I O S C O R V
N R I E M A I A P M E E C U O L O X
D E C N U A T V W F N G R O N L F R
B L M X O R O I R C I A A U I A B G
Q O H H M U U U N E P T T T C N S S
P H A N T A S M A G O R I A I U I K
C C Y L A M O N A R L O C F T N R M
E T A L U G N U X E N P W C E N B T
L A I V I V N O C S R K I W M N U P
Z V M Z A T H E I S T R Y Q E W H S
```

Anger (6)
Animal with hooves (8)
Carry or transport a boat over land (7)
Criticized; reproached (9)
Determination; will (8)
Disastrous (10)
Dominating; bossy; dictatorial (10)
Excess (7)
Excessively thin (5)
Extreme or exaggerated self-confidence (6)
Fantastic images seen as if in a dream (14)
Flooding; covering (10)
Foolish; ridiculous (7)
Intimidated; bullied (8)
Irregularity; exception (7)
Leniency; acceptance; tolerance (6)
Line or boundary that is irrevocable once it is crossed (7)

Loud; impressive (8)
Means of exit; a way out (6)
Mystery; something difficult to understand (6)
Nickname (9)
Of the lower class of society (6)
One who does not believe in God or any deity (7)
Open-mouthed grin (6)
Remarked; commented (6)
Search for food or provisions (6)
Social; enjoying feasting together & good company (9)
Someone who spies on another's personal life (6)
Something that causes vomiting (6)
Stringy but strong (6)
Threatening; foreboding (7)
Uncertainties (8)
Unqualified; pure (9)
Wangled; acquired through ingenuity (9)

ANSWER KEY VOCABULARY WORD SEARCH *Into the Wild*

```
S  O  N  O  R  O  U  S  I  N  V  E  I  G  L  E  D
I  D  E  R  O  T  C  E  H  T  E  U  Q  I  R  B  O  S
E  N  U  P  B  R  A  I  D  E  D     A     U  D  E
V  N  U           L  R  E  P  M  U  L  B  E  G
O  O  I  N        A  A  L  E  N  I  T  Y  I  Y  A
   M  Y  G  D     M  G        D  I  O  S  C  O  R  V
   R  I  E  M  A  I  A        E  E  C  U  O  L  O
   E     N  U  A  T  V     F  N  G  R  O  N  L  F
   L        O  R  O  I  R     I  A  A  U  I  A
   O           U  U  U  N  E  P  T  T  T  C  N  S  S
P  H  A  N  T  A  S  M  A  G  O  R  I  A  I  U  I
   C  Y  L  A  M  O  N  A  R     O  C  F  T  N  R
E  T  A  L  U  G  N  U     E  N  P     C  E     B
L  A  I  V  I  V  N  O  C  S           I  W  M  U
         A  T  H  E  I  S  T  R  Y        E     H
```

Anger (6)
Animal with hooves (8)
Carry or transport a boat over land (7)
Criticized; reproached (9)
Determination; will (8)
Disastrous (10)
Dominating; bossy; dictatorial (10)
Excess (7)
Excessively thin (5)
Extreme or exaggerated self-confidence (6)
Fantastic images seen as if in a dream (14)
Flooding; covering (10)
Foolish; ridiculous (7)
Intimidated; bullied (8)
Irregularity; exception (7)
Leniency; acceptance; tolerance (6)
Line or boundary that is irrevocable once it is crossed (7)

Loud; impressive (8)
Means of exit; a way out (6)
Mystery; something difficult to understand (6)
Nickname (9)
Of the lower class of society (6)
One who does not believe in God or any deity (7)
Open-mouthed grin (6)
Remarked; commented (6)
Search for food or provisions (6)
Social; enjoying feasting together & good company (9)
Someone who spies on another's personal life (6)
Something that causes vomiting (6)
Stringy but strong (6)
Threatening; foreboding (7)
Uncertainties (8)
Unqualified; pure (9)
Wangled; acquired through ingenuity (9)

VOCABULARY CROSSWORD *Into the Wild*

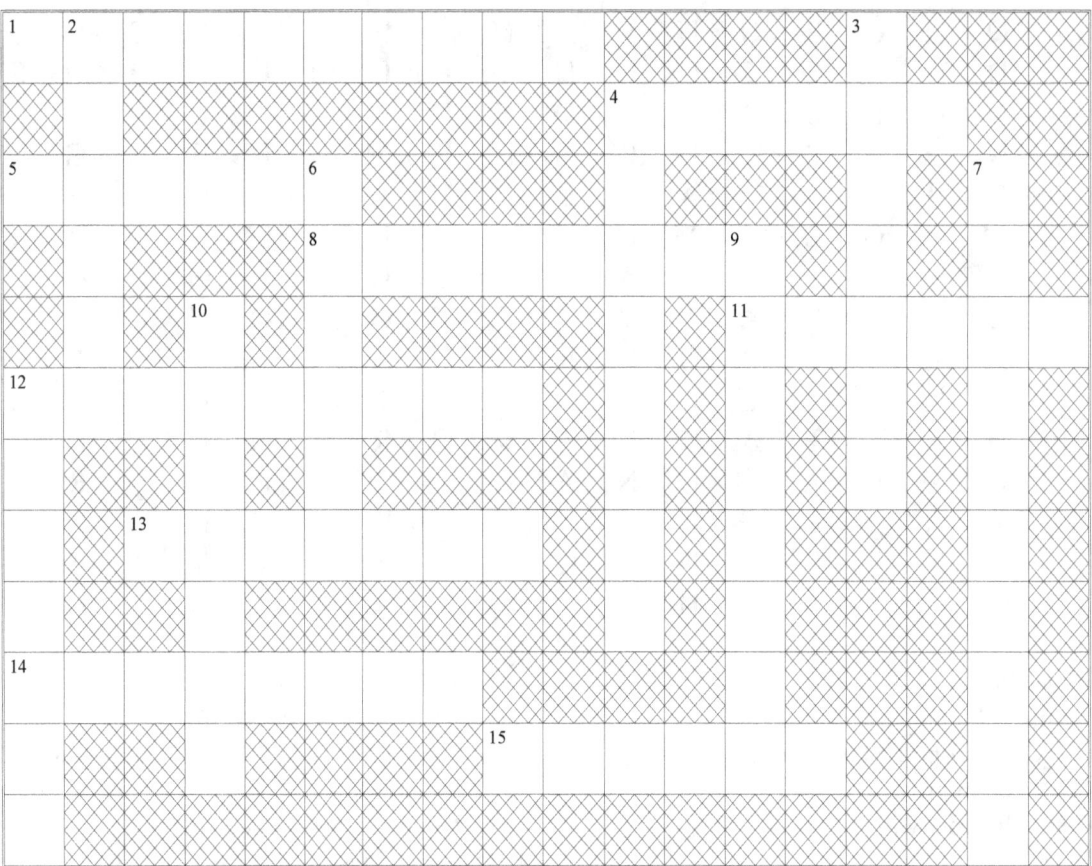

Across
1. Ability to be stretched out of shape and readily return to original form
4. Lack of; shortage
5. Something that causes vomiting
8. Intimidated; bullied
11. Mystery; something difficult to understand
12. Inconsistent
13. Burdensome
14. Walk; move from place to place
15. Means of exit; a way out

Down
2. Of the lower class of society
3. One who does not believe in God or any deity
4. Abandoned
6. Anger
7. Distinguishes; sets apart
9. Citizens; residents
10. Threatening; foreboding
12. Irregularity; exception

ANSWER KEY VOCABULARY CROSSWORD *Into the Wild*

	1	2											3	
	E	L	A	S	T	I	C	I	T	Y			A	
		U						4 D	E	A	R	T	H	
5 E	M	E	T	I	6 C			E			H		7 D
		P			8 H	E	C	T	O	9 R	E	D	E
			10							11				
		E	O		O			E		E	N	I	G	M	A
12 A	N	O	M	A	L	O	U	S		L		N	S		A
N			I		E			L		I		I	T		R
O		13 O	N	E	R	O	U	S		C		Z			C
M			O							T		E			A
14 A	M	B	U	L	A	T	E					N			T
L			S					15 E	G	R	E	S	S		E
Y															S

Across
1. Ability to be stretched out of shape and readily return to original form
4. Lack of; shortage
5. Something that causes vomiting
8. Intimidated; bullied
11. Mystery; something difficult to understand
12. Inconsistent
13. Burdensome
14. Walk; move from place to place
15. Means of exit; a way out

Down
2. Of the lower class of society
3. One who does not believe in God or any deity
4. Abandoned
6. Anger
7. Distinguishes; sets apart
9. Citizens; residents
10. Threatening; foreboding
12. Irregularity; exception

VOCABULARY MATCHING *Into the Wild*

____ 1. VOLITION   A. Line or boundary that is irrevocable once it is crossed

____ 2. MUNIFICENCE   B. Lack of; shortage

____ 3. LAMPOONED   C. Abundance; plenty

____ 4. SONOROUS   D. Burdensome

____ 5. ANOMALY   E. Fantastic images seen as if in a dream

____ 6. RUBICON   F. Satirized; ridiculed

____ 7. SUBCUTANEOUS   G. Eccentric; peculiar

____ 8. VERACITY   H. Irregularity; exception

____ 9. PHANTASMAGORIA   I. Reproached; rebuked

____ 10. INSIDIOUSLY   J. Scarcity

____ 11. EREMITIC   K. Unplanned; impromptu

____ 12. PAUCITY   L. Hermit-like; solitary

____ 13. DEARTH   M. Truth

____ 14. EXTEMPORANEOUS   N. Loud; impressive

____ 15. OPPROBRIUM   O. Determination; will

____ 16. ONEROUS   P. Citizens; residents

____ 17. IDIOSYNCRATIC   Q. Under the skin

____ 18. DENIZENS   R. Criticism; judgment

____ 19. EMOTIVE   S. Dangerously subtle; developing slowly until its too late

____ 20. CASTIGATED   T. Emotionally expressive

ANSWER KEY VOCABULARY MATCHING *Into the Wild*

O   1. VOLITION   A. Line or boundary that is irrevocable once it is crossed

C   2. MUNIFICENCE   B. Lack of; shortage

F   3. LAMPOONED   C. Abundance; plenty

N   4. SONOROUS   D. Burdensome

H   5. ANOMALY   E. Fantastic images seen as if in a dream

A   6. RUBICON   F. Satirized; ridiculed

Q   7. SUBCUTANEOUS   G. Eccentric; peculiar

M   8. VERACITY   H. Irregularity; exception

E   9. PHANTASMAGORIA   I. Reproached; rebuked

S   10. INSIDIOUSLY   J. Scarcity

L   11. EREMITIC   K. Unplanned; impromptu

J   12. PAUCITY   L. Hermit-like; solitary

B   13. DEARTH   M. Truth

K   14. EXTEMPORANEOUS   N. Loud; impressive

R   15. OPPROBRIUM   O. Determination; will

D   16. ONEROUS   P. Citizens; residents

G   17. IDIOSYNCRATIC   Q. Under the skin

P   18. DENIZENS   R. Criticism; judgment

T   19. EMOTIVE   S. Dangerously subtle; developing slowly until its too late

I   20. CASTIGATED   T. Emotionally expressive

VOCABULARY JUGGLE LETTERS *Into the Wild*

_____ = 1. SACGDTETIA
Reproached; rebuked

_____ = 2. ITESELP
Formal letter

_____ = 3. YSORIACCTDIIN
Eccentric; peculiar

_____ = 4. LAEBTMUA
Walk; move from place to place

_____ = 5. URBOCIN
Line or boundary that is irrevocable once it is crossed

_____ = 6. OHTEDRCE
Intimidated; bullied

_____ = 7. REOVYU
Someone who spies on another's personal life

_____ = 8. YISICTTLAE
Ability to be stretched out of shape and readily return to original form

_____ = 9. IMCRTEIE
Hermit-like; solitary

_____ =10. EAGTULUN
Animal with hooves

_____ =11. OMNAIAMNO
Excessive fixation on a single idea

_____ =12. GOCSESRN
The act of coming together

ANSWER KEY VOCABULARY JUGGLE LETTERS *Into the Wild*

CASTIGATED = 1. SACGDTETIA
Reproached; rebuked

EPISTLE = 2. ITESELP
Formal letter

IDIOSYNCRATIC = 3. YSORIACCTDIIN
Eccentric; peculiar

AMBULATE = 4. LAEBTMUA
Walk; move from place to place

RUBICON = 5. URBOCIN
Line or boundary that is irrevocable once it is crossed

HECTORED = 6. OHTEDRCE
Intimidated; bullied

VOYEUR = 7. REOVYU
Someone who spies on another's personal life

ELASTICITY = 8. YISICTTLAE
Ability to be stretched out of shape and readily return to original form

EREMITIC = 9. IMCRTEIE
Hermit-like; solitary

UNGULATE = 10. EAGTULUN
Animal with hooves

MONOMANIA = 11. OMNAIAMNO
Excessive fixation on a single idea

CONGRESS = 12. GOCSESRN
The act of coming together

www.ingramcontent.com/pod-product-compliance
Lightning Source LLC
Chambersburg PA
CBHW051406070526
44584CB00023B/3308